DEWEY W. GRANTHAM is Professor of History at
Vanderbilt University. He was born in Manassas,
Georgia and took his B. A. from the University of
Georgia in 1942. His M. A. (1947) and Ph. D. (1949)
were earned at the University of North Carolina. From
1955 to 1956 he was at Harvard as a fellow of the Fund
for the Advancement of Education. He taught at North
Texas State College and the Woman's College of the
University of North Carolina before coming to Vanderbilt in 1952. His reputation as a student of the history
of the South was recognized when the Southern Historical Association presented him its biennial Sydnor
Award for his book *Hoke Smith and the Politics of the
New South.* He has contributed regularly to scholarly
journals, and, in 1962, he was invited to deliver the
sixth series of the Lamar Memorial Lectures annually
given at Mercer University. These lectures are now
published as *The Democratic South.*

THE
DEMOCRATIC
SOUTH

DEWEY W. GRANTHAM, JR.

The Norton Library
W · W · NORTON & COMPANY · INC ·
NEW YORK

Eugenia Dorothy Blount Lamar
Memorial Lectures, 1962
Delivered at Mercer University on October 23, 24, 25

Books That Live
The Norton imprint on a book means that in the publisher's
estimation it is a book not for a single season but for the years.
W. W. Norton & Company, Inc.

PRINTED IN THE UNITED STATES OF AMERICA

2 3 4 5 6 7 8 9 0

FOR

MY MOTHER

IT WILL BE SOMETHING IF THESE PAPERS SHALL MAKE IT plain that my subject is a true body of human life,—a thing, and not a mass of facts, a topic in political science, an object lesson in large moralities. To know the thing itself should be our study; and the right study of it is thought and passion, not research alone. For this, like every other great and tragical human thing, passes forever into the mind and character and life of whosoever touches it, though he touch it never so lightly. If he himself be born of it, then he inherits all its past. It will forever strain him forth beyond his narrow bounds of individual experience; darken his doubt into bewilderment; insist upon its share in his achievement; echo with its Appomattox his little failures and surrenders.

WILLIAM GARROTT BROWN

Contents

Foreword

FEW HISTORIANS HAVE EVER BEEN CALLED UPON TO COMPETE with history quite as dramatically as was Dewey W. Grantham as he delivered his series of Lamar Lectures at Mercer University in late October of 1962. President Kennedy had just taught the world a new meaning of the word *quarantine;* normally unruffled citizens were purchasing cans of water and hastily stocking their basements with provisions; Soviet freighters were moving—seemingly inexorably—toward the U. S. naval blockade off Cuba. Professor Grantham's audiences came to him between anxious waits by the television sets, their minds on the impending showdown between the United States and the Soviet Union. But despite these distractions of cosmic proportions, the Grantham lectures—models of structural unity and sound scholarship—were heard and deeply appreciated. This distinguished young scholar, the first native Georgian to deliver a series of Lamar Lectures, skillfully delineated the forces that have interacted to encourage the South's attachment to the Democratic party. He also pointed out some interesting evidence of variety within the one-party milieu.

With the publication of this sixth series of Eugenia Dorothy Blount Lamar Memorial Lectures, the Lamar

Lecture Committee and Mercer University reaffirm their gratitude to the late Mrs. Lamar's wisdom and generosity in endowing this perpetual series of lectures. Mrs. Lamar, a cultural leader in Macon and the South for nearly three-quarters of a century, was keenly interested in the continuation of traditional Southern values amid the kaleidoscope of social and economic changes taking place in the modern South. She left a legacy to Mercer University with the request that it be used "to provide lectures of the very highest type of scholarship which will aid in the permanent preservation of the values of Southern culture, history, and literature."

BENJAMIN W. GRIFFITH, JR., *Chairman*
The Lamar Lecture Committee

Mercer University
Macon, Georgia

virtues of state rights and home rule. But it would be a mistake to assume that southern society and southern politics have been static during the last century. The economic and social revolution that is now under way in the South can best be understood as the phenomenal climax of deep-rooted and historic developments in the region and in the country as a whole. Those developments have had their impact on southern politics and in our own day they give promise of producing a more realistic and a more democratic politics for the South.

The interpretation of the Democratic South presented here grew out of a more intensive study of political and social reform in the southern states during the progressive era. The more I investigated the sources of southern progressivism and the nature of its impact during the first two decades of this century, the more convinced I became that our understanding of the extent to which the region experienced social conflict and adopted salutary reforms has been obscured by the myth of a monolithic and conservative South. This is not to deny the fundamental conservatism of the South, nor to minimize the importance of the institutionalization of one-party politics below the Potomac. Nevertheless, the events of this period make it abundantly clear that southern politics was far more than a politics of sectionalism and Negrophobia. Southerners were divided by real economic and social distinctions, and these differences sometimes were translated into political and social action. Furthermore, the politics of the individual southern states varied enormously and, like the state politics of the country as a whole, must be properly approached with an eye to richly diversified elements of historical circumstance and environmental character. Finally, the progressive movement in the South may have reflected far more than we realize the attitudes and aspirations of Americans generally, and also the way in which the events of these years grew out of and contributed to historic forces that were basically American. It is with this thought in mind that I have attempted in these lectures to outline the Democratic South.

I am grateful to the Lamar Lecture Committee for inviting me to take part in its distinguished lecture series, and to the students and faculty of Mercer University for the warm reception they gave me. I am particularly indebted to Professor Benjamin W. Griffith, Chairman of the Lamar Lecture Committee, to Professor Spencer B. King and the members of the Department of History and Government, and to Dean Robert H. Spiro for all they did to make my visit a memorable personal experience.

The errors of fact and interpretation in this volume are of course mine alone, but my obligations to other scholars are numerous and profound, and only partially suggested in the Bibliographical Note following the text. I owe a particularly heavy debt to two friends and colleagues at Vanderbilt University, Robert J. Harris and Henry Lee Swint. They generously read the manuscript in an early draft and gave me the benefit of their wide knowledge of southern politics and institutions. Mr. Charles F. Cummings, while serving as my research assistant, worked indefatigably in the scattered and incomplete election returns of the nineteenth century for the foundation on which some of my generalizations about southern politics rest. The counsel and friendship of Fletcher M. Green of the University of North Carolina in this, as in other scholarly ventures, have benefited and sustained me far more than he realizes. Finally, I am happy to acknowledge my lasting gratitude to my wife, Virginia Burleson Grantham, and to my mother, Ellen Holland Grantham, for services too great to measure. To the latter this book is affectionately dedicated.

Portions of these lectures appeared in a different form

in "An American Politics for the South," an essay in Charles Grier Sellers, Jr. (ed.), *The Southerner As American* (Chapel Hill, 1960). I wish to thank the University of North Carolina Press for permission to include them in this new version. The quotation from William Garrott Brown preceding the Preface is taken from Brown's *The Lower South in American History* (New York, 1902), and is used with the permission of the Macmillan Company.

My research has been aided by grants from the John Simon Guggenheim Memorial Foundation, the Institute of Research in the Social Sciences at Vanderbilt University, and the Social Science Research Council.

DEWEY W. GRANTHAM

Vanderbilt University
Nashville, Tennessee

who have long viewed the landscape from afar, and that even the inhabitants of the unknown country discount its geographical diversities and variegated natural life as irrelevant in the face of the land's boldest and most harmonious features.

This fanciful statement will perhaps suggest that an important element in the study of southern political history should be the critique of myths. It has become increasingly clear from the researches of C. Vann Woodward, V. O. Key, Jr., and many others that southern society has always been more complex, differentiated, and internally at odds than myth would indicate, and that the issues and cleavages in southern politics have more often than not been those found in other parts of the country. Yet the myth of the "Solid South" persists, and few serious historians would deny that for over a century it has been a significant factor in American history. The historian would disregard it at his peril, for however much myths conceal and distort, the symbols and images they project often reveal fundamental values and aspirations.

The South, as the peculiar child in the family of American sections, has certainly been susceptible to myth-making. Because its history has differed in important respects from the rest of the nation, Southerners and other Americans have created what Professor Woodward describes as an "elaborate myth"—or mythology—about the region. But there are also national myths. It may be that the American mythology about the "conservative South," for example, contains within it an equally powerful myth concerning American democracy, and that the southern symbolism has its national uses. The idea of the Solid South long ago became a handy stereotype, a symbol of an aberrant sectionalism in a healthy America. The significant point is that the nation's democratic ideals and practices came to be defined, in no small part, in terms of what was popularly assumed to be the antithesis of southern ideals and practices. Even in the historical writing on America's great sectional conflict, suggests David M. Potter, "the quest for an unqualified antithesis still continues." Yet there is some doubt that the South was any more conservative than other parts of the country during such a period as the Gilded Age, and there is abundant evidence that it was more liberal than many other sections during the Populist era. Perhaps Americans —so pragmatic, so lacking in political ideology, and yet so dynamic—needed the comforting illusion of a fundamental and continuing struggle in the inevitable progression toward the democratic millennium. Or perhaps the South became a sort of scapegoat because of the psychological stresses and strains resulting from the discrepancy between American political practices and the American ideal of the equality of man. At any rate, southern sectionalism provided much of the grist for the ideological mills of American democracy. This is not to say that southern sectionalism lacked solid foundations, nor to imply that the image of the "conservative South" was created primarily by non-Southerners. But to overlook the national implications of the symbol is to overlook one of the important reasons for its remarkable vitality and to miss some of the significance in an important chapter in the history of American politics.

Southern sectionalism arose out of real economic and cultural differences that increasingly separated Southerners and Northerners, but it is easy to exaggerate those differences and especially so in the post-Civil War period. Americans have experienced plenty of social conflict but much of its meaning is lost when it is presented in terms of a clash between monolithic sections. "The conflicts that have been so much a part of the southern experience," writes Charles G. Sellers, "have occurred . . . between

Southerners and within Southerners, as much as between North and South." Emphasis upon the need for a valid critique of this part of the southern mythology does not mean denial of the fundamental conservatism of southern politics. Certainly in the nineteenth century the South fell far short of realizing the democratic ideals of representative political institutions based on manhood suffrage, the ultimate rule of the majority, equal protection under the law, and what de Tocqueville called "equality of condition." But eloquent statement of the ideal rather than realization of it was common almost everywhere in nineteenth-century America.

There has been a "democratic South" as well as a "conservative South." A sound and realistic history of southern life and institutions must rest upon an understanding and a proper evaluation of this fact. In one sense, of course, the "Democratic South" is part and parcel of the Solid South myth, for it provides a convenient symbol to describe the region's fidelity to a single party during the long period since Reconstruction. But in another sense it refers to forces that often ran counter to the dominance of the Democratic party and the political unity of the section. The term is used here both to designate the South's long attachment to the Democratic party and, in a more fundamental sense, to describe those ideas and practices of a "democratic" nature that have manifested themselves in southern politics since the inception of the Solid South. By examining in historical perspective the clash between the centripetal forces promoting political unity and the centrifugal forces threatening to disrupt the Solid South, it may be possible to get some notion of the extent and vitality of the "democratic South," as well as a better understanding of the region's politics in general.

Any evaluation of the democratic elements in southern politics should begin with some reference to the fact that politics in the South has continually reflected definite groups within the social structure and geography of the region. A study of what one writer has called "the natural history of southern society" makes increasingly clear the fact that the basic ingredients of southern politics have been, not doctrines of race, but socio-economic groupings not unlike those outside the section—business-minded conservatives, agrarian radicals, middle-class progressives, and the like. The groupings may have lacked the diversity and vitality found in many other areas, but it would be a serious mistake to discount them altogether.

Recurrent social and economic cleavages have been present in virtually all of the political crises experienced by the South—in the interparty competition of the Old South, in the struggle over secession and southern independence, in the agrarian revolt, and in the factionalism of southern politics in the twentieth century. A recent study of political tendencies in Louisiana reveals that the politics of modern Louisiana is grounded in identifiable social and economic distinctions in the population, and that many of these elements have a political significance stretching back well over a century. Roger W. Shugg, searching for the roots of the social upheaval that attended Populism, found in an earlier study that "objective" classes in Louisiana had long been in conflict. The central theme in Mississippi politics for fifty years following Reconstruction, writes another historian, "is a struggle between economic classes, interspersed with the personal struggles of ambitious men." No matter how assiduously they played upon the themes of race and tradition, the advocates of sectional solidarity were never able to impose sufficient unity on the white majority to override for long the fundamental pattern of group conflict. With the passage of time the character of the competing groups inevitably changed, and in the process altered the main currents in southern politics.

Although these divisions asserted themselves wherever social and economic differences existed, there were definite geographical patterns in their manifestation. One such pattern grew out of the economic and cultural differences among the subregions of every state—whether it be the sectional struggle between the eastern plains and the western hills in Virginia and the Carolinas or the delta versus the hills and piney woods in Mississippi, Louisiana, and Arkansas. A second geographical division within the South involved broader cleavages. Important distinctions began to appear early between the Southwest and the older Atlantic seaboard states, and it is not without significance that in our own day Texas and Oklahoma are becoming more and more western in outlook. More important, however, was the growing economic and political conflict between the upper and the lower South. The behavior of the upper South in the secession crisis points up a persistent theme in the politics of the region: it has always been a divisive element in southern politics. Having a more diversified economy, one that was more nationally integrated, that part of the South resisted political unification in 1861 and in the years that followed.

A second major element in the democratic basis of southern politics is the region's participation in what Fletcher M. Green has aptly called the great cycles of American democracy. Southerners have never really been isolated from the larger American scene, nor have they been oblivious to the prevailing currents in national thought. For the South was American before it was southern, and the most important fact about the Southerner is that he has been throughout his history also an American. It has sometimes seemed that the "southern way" would become the American way, but the opposite was usually the case, and however bitter their protests and however keen their rationalizations, most Southerners have always been eager for the approbation of other Americans and large numbers of them have been ready to associate themselves with America's democratic ideals.

Southerners were powerfully affected by the equalitarian ideals of the Revolution—the doctrines of natural rights, popular sovereignty, government by contract, and the perfectibility of man. They drank deeply at the fount of America's triumphant nationalism. Many of these "Americans below the Potomac" responded in a positive manner to the political ideas of Thomas Jefferson and a great host of them gave staunch support to the democracy of Andrew Jackson. The revolutionary tradition of liberty did not die among such men, and the themes of democracy and individualism were constantly manifested in their politics and social views. Not even Radical Reconstruction was without its ideological supporters in the white South, for a substantial number of old Whigs and lower-class white men joined with "Carpetbaggers" and Negroes (themselves Southerners!) to carry out the most sweeping extension of political democracy the region had ever known. Although their democratic achievements and equalitarian ideals soon became the object of contempt and revulsion among white Southerners, these reform-minded men of the South made a lasting contribution to the democratic tradition in America. It is one of the little ironies of southern history that the ideals these Reconstruction reformers sought to implement are essentially the same ideals that inspire a larger number of Americans during the "New Reconstruction" we are now witnessing.

Eventually, the South's racial aberration and one-party politics set it apart from the rest of the nation, but the region below the Potomac was never able to repudiate its Americanism. As Louis Hartz has said, "When the guns of the Civil War were stilled the liberal self that the South could not sublimate even in the age of its great 'reaction' would gradually come to the fore again and, as in the days of Jefferson, would unite it to the North." Southerners, like other Americans, believed in the Christian dogma, in the doctrine of progress, and in the ideal of equality—by which they usually meant equality of economic opportunity. Many Southerners were painfully aware of the paradox involved in the existence of slavery in a land of liberty. The fact that the southern concept of democracy was heavily weighted with the ballast of materialism and that the North embarked for a season upon an egalitarian vessel should not obscure the basic agreement in the views of the protagonists. The point is that democracy in America has always been an unfinished business, evolving and being reformulated with the passage of time. In the nineteenth century most Americans found it difficult to include non-white elements in their democratic ideals, and Northerners as well as Southerners were usually prepared to surrender the broader implications of their democracy when they seemed to interfere with economic opportunities and materialistic progress. Even so, says Francis B. Simkins, Jefferson's Declaration of Independence "was destined to haunt the good Southerner during his deeds of darkest reaction and to inspire him with ideals of greater democracy in his hopeful moments."

A third component in the democratic basis of southern politics is the operation of the American federal system. It has simply not been possible for the South to avoid the integrating effects of the federal system—and its inhabitants have not always wanted to avoid them. As William R. Taylor has suggested in another connection, during most of its history the South has carried on a kind of dialogue with the nation at large. The more spectacular episodes in the dialecticism this dialogue reflected—nullification, secession, Reconstruction, and rhetorical state rights—tend to obscure the way in which the changing nature of American federalism has steadily pulled the region toward national involvement. The party system, for one thing, even when one party dominated a state or region, has proved a mighty barrier against the isolation of state politics. Evidence of this fact is to be found on every hand: in the efforts of the Old South to co-operate with the West, in the Bourbon alliance with the Northeast in the post-Reconstruction era, in the attempts of southern agrarians to make common cause with western farmers during the Populist era and to some extent during the 1920's, in the so-called southern Democratic-Republican coalition of modern times, and in the response of southern liberals throughout our history to the leadership of national leaders bent on social reform.

Such a leader as Andrew Jackson was sometimes more popular among Southerners than was his program but the result, in any case, was the introduction of divisive issues from the outside into internal politics and the appearance of national pressures to counter particularistic tendencies. Although most Southerners since Reconstruction have been slavish supporters of the Democratic party, they have been forced to use bifocal lenses in viewing their party; and, inevitably, their behavior as Democrats—even in their local politics—has reflected the leadership and ideology of the party on the national level. The leadership of William Jennings Bryan, Woodrow Wilson, and Franklin D. Roosevelt served to democratize and nationalize politics in the modern South, providing Southerners with an opportunity for at least a vicarious participation in national affairs and a sense of democratic fulfillment that transcended parochial attachments.

The growing centralization of power and the decline of localism in the recent period of United States history is, of course, the most notable aspect of the changing character of American federalism. The two sides of centralization represent different symbols to Southerners—and to other

Americans as well—but both sides have left their mark on southern politics. One side of the coin represents federal intervention or threatened intervention in the political process at the state and local levels. Such interference more often than not served the interests of white solidarity, and for a long time southern politicians could profitably brandish the possibility of federal "meddling" without any serious likelihood of actual intervention. But the realities of national coercion began to manifest themselves during the New Deal and dramatically so with the opening of white primaries to Negro voters by the Supreme Court in *Smith v. Allwright* (1944). The other side of the coin symbolizes the federal government as the source of appropriations and welfare legislation which state and local governments cannot or will not provide. Not all Southerners approve of this symbol, but few have shown any eagerness to turn down their share of the federal largess, and disadvantaged groups from the insurgent farmers of the late nineteenth century to the labor and Negro organizations of the mid-twentieth have increasingly turned to Washington rather than to Richmond or Jackson for help in realizing their objectives.

If these observations are sound, political democracy in the South rests on a foundation made up of three major elements: socio-economic groupings similar to those outside the region, the democratic ideology shared by all Americans, and the nation's constitutional system and the party practices that have developed under that system. To illustrate the early interaction of these elements in southern politics, let us turn for a moment to that fabled land of legend, the Old South.

As a matter of fact, that particular legend has fallen on evil days—its luster has dimmed. Modern scholars have shown that the Old South was never a monolithic entity and that it nourished a rather hardy strain of democracy. For one thing, it was too commercial minded, too bourgeois, to be at war with America's democratic-capitalistic system. Despite the growing stratification of society in the ante-bellum South, a genuine aristocracy never developed. Cheap land was too abundant. It provided the basis for a vigorous and independent yeoman class—largely landowners and diversified farmers. Although the "leathershirt class" was never adequately represented in the political life of the time and increasingly came under the political sway of planter-politicians, it nevertheless provided much of the support for a lively two-party system. During the first half of the nineteenth century, the common man in the South as in other parts of the country awoke to a new political consciousness, joined the party of Andrew Jackson, demanded his political rights as a free man, and began to turn to the state for new services. Many of these yeomen, especially those outside of the "black belts" and delta areas, remained more nationalistic in attitude and more devoted to Jacksonian principles than their wealthier slaveholding contemporaries in the fertile lowlands. Whether of Democratic or Whig persuasion in 1860-61, these were the men who furnished much of the opposition to secession and who, in the years following the great sectional conflict, lent support to independent and insurgent movements that opened fissures in Democratic solidarity.

The geographical differences existing in most southern states and the political conflicts growing out of social and economic distinctions were strikingly evident in the constitutional reforms achieved in the South during the period 1800-1860. These democratic advances also reflected the force of the democratic ideology that was being implemented during the generation before the Civil War. Despite the stubborn opposition of conservative leaders and the groups they represented, almost every southern state gradually revised its constitution so that substantial political equality for white men existed. The suffrage was extended to virtually all white men, most officers were elected by popular vote, representation was equalized, property qualifications for officeholding were abolished, and local government was made more democratic.

The ideals of Jacksonian democracy infused the new state constitutions, and the governments under them began to concern themselves with the needs and aspirations of a larger percentage of white citizens. A considerable number of yeoman farmers began to enter politics, in part no doubt because of social mobility made possible by economic opportunities. Ironically, the growth of southern nationalism and the drive for conformity in support of sectional ideals in the 1850's may have encouraged the expansion of democracy among white Southerners, since the advocates of a unanimous South found it helpful, in discoursing on the political equality of white men in the Cotton Kingdom, to demonstrate their good faith with tangible evidence. At any rate, the percentage of white people voting and the balanced nature of the bipartisan politics in the ante-bellum South approximated the situation in other parts of the country.

If the small farmers in the ante-bellum period tended to follow Jeffersonian and Jacksonian precepts and to enter the Democratic party, the planters in most southern states became opponents of Jackson and supporters of the Whig party. The southern Whigs, as Charles G. Sellers has pointed out, represented far more than a state-rights aggregation of great planters. Their commercial affiliations, their policy positions on such issues as tariff and banking legislation, and their conservative reaction to the leveling tendencies of the day, marked them as natural followers of Henry Clay and as practitioners of national Whiggery. The persistence of these Whiggish attitudes was revealed in the secession crisis, when the old Whigs, particularly in the upper South, tended to oppose secession and favor co-operation and delay; in the politics of the Confederacy; and in the remarkable strength the old-line Whigs demonstrated at the war's end, when they virtually replaced the party of secession and war as the dominant element in southern political affairs. Whiggery also manifested itself in the kaleidoscopic phases of Reconstruction and the evolution of a southern consensus that would support redemption; in the industrialization of the region and the popularity of the "New South" ideology; and, to a great but as yet undetermined extent, in the politics of the modern South.

To return to the critique of myths: the myth of the "conservative South," like most myths, contains an element of truth. There is indeed a conservative tradition in the South and it is perhaps the region's dominant tradition, but where the symbolism goes farthest astray is in its implication that southern conservatism was somehow different from conservatism elsewhere in America. After all, there was a South of John Marshall and Henry Clay as well as a South of John C. Calhoun. The truth of the matter is that conservatism south of the Potomac owes far less to Calhoun than it does to the Bourbon Democrats who made peace with modern America in the 1870's and 1880's.

As for the Solid South stereotype, it too possesses an undeniable measure of truth. But like the myth of the "conservative South," it implies that sectional attitudes and one-party politics were peculiar to the South, when, in fact, they were prevalent in many other parts of the country, particularly during the last quarter of the nineteenth century. Lest it be thought that conflict within southern society is being overemphasized, it must be conceded that the unities in the region were, indeed, very great. There was clearly some kind of unity underlying southern sectionalism, but the most powerful unities were national rather than sectional in their scope. Our long fascination with

LECTURE
TWO

The Forging of the Solid South

BY THE MIDDLE OF THE NINETEENTH CENTURY, CHARLES S.
Sydnor wrote, "Southerners had come a long way from
Jefferson and a long way out of reality." Certainly the
South had begun to diverge in its course from that of the
North. Although the region had made striking gains in
population and wealth and had experienced in some measure most of the forces reshaping the nation's society, it had
changed far less than the northern part of the country. Its
economy, its society, its cultural attainments, its politics,
its very way of life seemed to provide an increasing con-
trast to the North, and Southerners were quick to see that
in almost all respects the section north of the Potomac and
the Ohio was outdistancing their own. The slavery controversy, the obsessive concern with the society of the rival
sections, and the introduction of moral issues into the
debate contributed to the hardening of sectional lines.
Perhaps the South's self-consciousness rested on a kind of
fictional sociology; perhaps its people were driven to des-

15

perate measures by half-doubts and internal conflicts they could repress in no other way. But no matter. Whether true or not, the idea had become widespread by 1860 that Southerners were a distinctive people in the American nation. It was surely this idea and this ideal that inspired those who fought for the Confederacy in the 1860's.

In most respects the exaggerated sectionalism of the late ante-bellum period served as a powerful damper on the furnace of southern democracy. Yet this sectionalism was itself the result in no small part of a democratic system. The enthronement of King Cotton, for example, was to some extent a consequence of the democratization of the lower South. Cotton was no discriminator against the common man in this area and ordinary men could achieve wealth and social status by climbing a stairway of cotton bales. Such an economic system encouraged concentrated wealth and social distinctions but the system was not very old in 1860. Perhaps it is significant to note that many of those whose rise to influence demonstrated the reality of economic opportunity and vertical mobility seemed eager to prove the existence of an old and well-developed status system. Yet the men who voted for secession were the products of a politics that was surprisingly democratic. Indeed, the very suddenness of the political revolution in some southern states may account for the paucity of legislative accomplishments and the accession to power of men unable to meet the needs of the time.

But the representative quality of southern politics in the late ante-bellum period must not be overemphasized. In the first place, if the distribution of political power was broadened and equalized in the Old South, it nevertheless remained true that the squirearchy, especially in the older states, exerted a disproportionate influence through its control of the county courts, the party caucuses, and the state legislatures. The planters and their commercial-lawyer allies kept taxes low and prevented the development of genuine public education programs. This became a massive roadblock in the progress of the common man in the South, as did the geographic and economic isolation of those yeomen who lived in the mountains and more remote areas. The unhappy result more often than not was a near-subsistence economy, a pervasive ignorance, and an extreme cultural provincialism. How could democracy thrive under such conditions? Moreover, the lack of class consciousness was strengthened by family ties between planter and yeoman, and by the incessant distinctions made on the basis of caste. Although only about one-fourth of the southern families owned slaves in 1860—and few of those owned very many—slavery nevertheless was the keystone in the arch of southern society, the source of social stratification among white Southerners but paradoxically the solvent of strong class consciousness. There is no avoiding the fact, Louis Hartz concludes, "that one of the crucial factors in the solidarity of the South was a democratic spirit enhanced by the slavery on which it rested."

In the second place, the unity Southerners achieved in the 1850's was bought at the price of freely competing parties, at least in terms of national organizations. In some states an internal rivalry within the Democratic party became more important by 1840 than Whig-Democratic competition, thus adumbrating the pattern of one-party contests in the Solid South following Reconstruction. The one-party trend had proceeded far enough in some states as early as 1850 to give a single party overwhelming control, and the remnants of an organized two-party system were rapidly destroyed in most other southern states by the late 1850's. The significant point about the two-party system in the Old South is not that Southerners abandoned their devotion to the principles espoused by the two parties, but that an elaborate and durable party machinery never developed. The two-party system never became institutionalized.

Finally and tragically, southern politics became increasingly provincial in its outlook, abandoning much of its Jeffersonian and Jacksonian heritage while seizing on the negative statesmanship of John C. Calhoun and the principle of state rights. Although Jefferson was not forgotten, only one side of his thought received much attention, that which emphasized individualism, personal liberty, and opposition to centralized power. Southern reactionaries, with all their talk about Greek democracy, would in fact dilute the region's democracy, challenge the ideal of political equality, concoct sophistries against majority rule, and proscribe many contemporary reforms associated with Yankee-American politics.

Even so, the secession movement was strongly opposed by many people in the South, especially in the upper part of the region. But to no avail. Southern destinies were controlled in the crisis by the areas of greatest fertility, per capita wealth, and slave population. Some of these sections had been Whig strongholds in earlier years but, whatever their antecedents, they had become secessionist in sentiment and generally Democratic in party affiliation. Representing the wealthiest and most powerful parts of the South, the party that had once been led by Jefferson and Jackson had by 1861 become the party of nullification, secession, and radical action. With power and leadership at its disposal, and with the help of events, it had taken a long stride toward the solidification of the South, even though many Southerners from less fertile regions found much to criticize in the leadership and program of the new southern Democracy.

But the Democrats were never able to achieve anything like complete unity, and opposition to their Confederate policies, primarily by old Whigs, increased as the war progressed. Indeed, the collapse of the Confederacy was probably made inevitable by the lack of enthusiasm on the part of great numbers of old Whigs and Union sympathizers for a Democratic war which many considered the height of folly. The Whiggish element turned increasingly toward peace and reconstruction schemes as the fortunes of the Confederacy declined, and when the war ended they replaced the discredited Democrats in such thoroughgoing fashion as to dominate southern politics in 1865-1866. Such opposition during the war reflected the democratic tendencies of the Confederacy: the democratic individualism of the southern soldier, the libertarian record of the Confederate government, and the political democracy that continued to prevail under the new regime. It is even possible to argue, as David Donald does, that the Confederacy "Died of Democracy." Yet the war itself provided indispensable material for sectional unity in the years that followed Appomattox. "We may say," observes Robert Penn Warren, "that only at the moment when Lee handed Grant his sword was the Confederacy born; or to state matters another way, in the moment of death the Confederacy entered upon its immortality."

Unfortunately, the southern Whigs were unable to maintain themselves in power and they gradually lost their identity as a separate group. The way in which this happened was complicated and the details are not yet clear. The Whigs differed among themselves as to policy, and while some of them lent their support to Radical Reconstruction and others attempted to retain their integrity as old-line Whigs by eschewing political involvement, they were ultimately driven by their frustration into the arms of the Democrats whose policies they had so often condemned. Thomas B. Alexander, the leading student of the Whigs, believes that the southern Whigs had a real opportunity immediately after the war to revive their party and take the lead in a moderate reconstruction program. He suggests that they failed to bring this about in part because of their own divided counsels and mistaken tactics, but also because of the inexplicable failure of conservative Republicans in the North to understand the real nature of political control in the South after the war. The situation was complicated by the historic accident that brought Andrew Johnson, a Southerner and a unionist but also a Democrat, to the presidency. Neither southern Whig nor northern Republican could bring himself to trust Johnson, since both suspected that he might be the instrument for the rejuvenation of the national Democratic party.

If Radical Reconstruction frustrated the southern Whigs in their efforts to reconstruct the South along moderate lines and if it ultimately destroyed the group as a clearly-recognizable entity, it did so by polarizing sentiment in the South and by rehabilitating the Democrats in the eyes of most white Southerners. Immediately after the war the Democrats had become men of humility. As the editor of the *Hinds County Gazette* of Mississippi wrote: "They wore sack-cloth. They heaped several bushels of ashes on their heads. They took back seats, muttering, in broken accents, 'We made a great mistake in secession.' " But this season of contrition passed and within a few years they began "to look fierce and talk big like they did before. They venture to mention Tom. Jefferson, John C. Calhoun and Jeff Davis!!" Meanwhile, the Radicals in the South alienated many of the old Whigs, who held their noses at the corruption and fraud, backed away from egalitarian experiments, and resented the personal affronts they sometimes suffered. The middle ground assumed by many southern moderates became increasingly untenable. "The circumstances now surrounding the *South*," declared an old Whig in Mississippi in 1868, ". . . are of such vast importance, and the lines so fairly drawn between the Radicals and Democrats, that the Whigs of the South cannot do otherwise than vote with the Democrats, though they do so under protest." This man could never quite trust the Democrats, yet by the end of Reconstruction he was urging all Southerners "to repair promptly and manfully to the polls and vote the nominated Democratic-Conservative Ticket—all of it, State, County and District."

Professor Woodward, in his illuminating study of the Compromise of 1877, has shown the influential role of the conservative old-line Whigs in the South in reaching an understanding with conservative Republicans for the ending of Radical Reconstruction in the last three states of the region. The termination of Reconstruction on the basis of Rutherford B. Hayes's program indicated that Republican leaders in the North had finally come to understand the potential value of the Whiggish elements in the South. But their overtures came too late to allow many southern Whigs to enter the Republican party, even though that party once more had become the party of Henry Clay. Too many ex-Whigs had compromised their independence by co-operating with the Democrats in opposing Radical rule. Furthermore, they had exacted a price for their support of the Democratic party—in many states they even forced the adoption of a new name for the party, usually the "Conservative party." Democratic leaders, faced with agrarian dissensions and threats from independents, were prepared to make concessions.

There was clearly evident by the end of Reconstruction an unprecedented degree of unity among white Southerners. It was enormously strengthened by the Redeemers' version of Reconstruction. They told a grim story of human suffering and of the southern battle for civilization during Reconstruction, and their story became an article of faith in the household of almost every white Southerner. "The slaughter and the sacrifices during our great civil war were terrible indeed," declared Representative Hilary A. Herbert of Alabama in 1890, "but those dark days were lighted by the shining valor of the patriot soldier; the storm clouds were gilded with glory." In Reconstruction, on the other hand, Herbert could find "nothing but wretchedness and humiliation, and shame, and crime begetting crime. There was no single redeeming feature, except the heroic determination of the better classes in the several states to restore good government." "We are a forgiving people," wrote a South Carolinian some years later, "and these crimes against civilization may be forgiven but will never be forgotten. No historian of the period yet has had the courage to paint this shameful picture of conquest and crime in true colors." There was a kind of folk quality in such widely-shared images of sectional oppression. In many of its aspects the actual process of Reconstruction was far different from the myth about it that developed during this period. But the illusions in the mind of the white Southerner were more important than the realities.

How can this myth-making be explained? Hardships and defeats and real or fancied wrongs no doubt contributed to such a retreat from reality. The economic outlook was hardly conducive to an unbridled optimism, and the region's manifold disadvantages in this respect seemed all the greater when contrasted with the burgeoning economy of the buoyant North. Where now was mighty King Cotton? But the South's defensiveness and self-consciousness rested on more than economic limitations. Perhaps, as T. Harry Williams contends, there was a peculiarly unreal and romantic quality in the way Southerners saw themselves and the world. Certainly the region's cultural distinctiveness and the mystical bonds of white fellowship brought white Southerners into closer communion during this time of alleged threats from "inferior" black men. Conservatism, as a southern scholar once wrote in the case of post-bellum Virginia, "was not only a political party, it was also a social code and a state of mind. . . ." Regardless of their origins, the Reconstruction mythology and the cultural unity that encouraged it supplied a good part of the foundation for the Solid South in politics.

During the late 1870's and the decade of the 1880's the politics of most southern states was dominated by the so-called Bourbon Democrats. The Bourbons were not unlike their conservative counterparts, Democratic and Republican, who dominated northern politics in this period. Although they paid homage to the beautiful and the brave in the ante-bellum South and identified themselves with the romantic cult of the Confederacy and the overthrow of Radical "misrule," they were convinced that economic progress would provide a solution to the South's problems. They became ardent advocates of investments below the Potomac, of southern industrialization, and of sectional reconciliation. Their hegemony reflected the corporate and financial interests in the South, especially those involved in railroad promotion, merchandising, and banking. The state governments under their leadership reduced taxes, starved public service agencies and eleemosynary institutions, and made economy in government a cardinal virtue. They celebrated laissez faire as warmly as any robber baron, yet they also advocated railroad subsidies and tax exemption for the new industries. They worked hard to perpetuate the Solid South, or at least the illusion of its solidarity, and they perfected a working alliance with eastern conservatives in national politics. While they did not absolutely proscribe Negro participation in politics, they characterized themselves as the defenders of white supremacy and, in their efforts to overcome the independents and dissenters who occasionally challenged their rule, their use of the race question took on the quality of a fine art. As Albert D. Kirwan says of the situation in Mississippi, they used the Negro "unsparingly to crush all incipient revolts against their authority."

The bulwark of the Bourbon control was the black belts, the historic centers of southern wealth and influence. Black-belt leaders found powerful allies in river towns and piedmont industrial centers, whose spokesmen represented the commercial and bourgeois elements associated with the "New South" movement. The yeomen farmers and ordinary workingmen, while usually supporters of the Democratic party, found themselves without much political influence. One reason for this development was the fact that many southern states continued the Reconstruction policy of basing legislative apportionment (and in turn representation in party conventions) on total population. This had the effect of removing white counties from control of some states at the same time the plantation belts were progressively restricting the political participation of the very elements that accounted for their numerical predominance. The disproportionate influence of the plantation element and rising commercial interests in an atmosphere of minimum government and niggardly appropriations rendered the small farmers and lower classes generally almost impotent in matters of state legislation, while the "courthouse rings" dominated by the planter-merchant-lawyer combines meant that public policy on the local level seldom served the interests of poor men. The result, in a period of chronic agricultural distress and increasing tenancy, was growing political apathy and, under that, sullen resentment.

There were, of course, some Southerners who called themselves Republicans. These men who belonged to the party of Lincoln in the post-Reconstruction years were largely of two greatly different and often mutually antagonistic types: the freedmen, who for the most part lived in the low country, and the white inhabitants of the southern mountains, who had not been slaveholders and had opposed secession.

Although every southern state supported the Democratic presidential ticket in 1880—the date usually given as marking the first clear-cut emergence of the Solid South—it is a mistake to assume that Republican strength drastically declined during the last two decades of the nineteenth century. The Republican percentage of the total presidential vote cast in the eleven ex-Confederate states in 1880 (over 40 per cent) was actually a little greater than that of 1876. The Republicans continued to show strength in 1884, when their ticket received a larger proportional vote than in 1880 in all but three of the ex-Confederate states. There was a general decline in Republican percentages below the Potomac in 1888 but only two or three southern states experienced a sharp drop over the previous election. Indeed, Republicanism remained a strong force in many southern states in the 1890's, and only after 1900 did a sharp falling off of Republican percentages take place throughout the region. Meanwhile, an occasional Republican congressman was elected from such states as South Carolina, Florida, Louisiana, and Texas; in the upper South a surprising number of Republican nominees won congressional seats, especially in the decade of the nineties, and party contests for some state offices remained quite competitive.

Some further analysis of Republican strength in national elections will perhaps illuminate more clearly this forgotten chapter of southern political history. In the three border states of Kentucky, West Virginia, and Maryland, which the Democrats carried in every presidential election between 1876 and 1892, the Republican party was always strong, and increasingly so after the early nineties. All three states went Republican in 1896, and the Grand Old Party dominated their congressional delegations in the late nineties while winning the governorship at least once in each commonwealth. Of the more distinctly southern states, Virginia, North Carolina, and Tennessee were a political battleground between the two major parties in almost every election. The Republican percentage of the presidential vote in Virginia during the period 1876-1900 was never less than 39 per cent, and in 1884 and 1888 it was 49 per cent. During the same period North Carolina Republicans dropped below 46 per cent only once—with 36 per cent of the total vote in 1892 (the Populist ticket obtained 16 per cent). In Tennessee, meanwhile, the Republicans received at least 44 per cent of the presidential votes in every election except in 1876 and 1892, when their proportion of the popular vote dropped just below 40 per cent. Tennessee and North Carolina elected Republican governors during the period, and each of the three states sent Republican congressmen to Washington, sometimes five or six at once.

In another group of southern states—Alabama, Arkansas, Georgia, and Texas—Republican presidential strength was greater during the period 1876-1900 than is usually recognized, hovering around one-third of the total vote. As late as 1900 the Republican percentage of the vote was 35 per cent in Alabama and Arkansas, 28 per cent in Georgia, and 31 per cent in Texas. In Florida the Republican percentage was 40 or more in every election through 1888, after which it dropped to a steady level of about 20 per cent. The decline in Louisiana began four years earlier, dropping from 42 per cent in 1884 to 27 per cent in 1888 and gradually sinking to 20 per cent in 1900. Mississippi Republicanism showed the same pattern, declining from 36 per cent of the total votes cast in 1884 to 25 per cent in 1888, and reaching 10 per cent in 1900. The South Carolina percentage declined steadily throughout the period, from 34 per cent in 1880 to 9 per cent in 1900.

It should be remarked that the Republicans lost strength constantly in the black belts during the 1880's—a reflection perhaps of the success Whiggish elements were having in the Bourbon Democracy of the period. The fact that South Carolina, Mississippi, and Louisiana were the earliest southern states to show a sharp diminution in Republican voting percentages lends weight to this supposition. Although Republican losses in the black belts resulted in part from the manipulation and intimidation of Negro voters, they also resulted from the lessening attraction of Republicanism to southern whites who might logically have entered that party. Josephus Daniels, a fledgling newspaper editor in North Carolina during the Bourbon years, later quoted some of the old-time Democrats as saying: "We had to get the old Whigs in by using a good deal of soft soap, but after we got them in, they were better Democrats than we were and got most of the offices." The point to be kept in mind is that Republicanism in national elections did not become insignificant in most southern states until after 1900, and even then it remained strong enough in several states to influence the behavior of the dominant party.

The success achieved by the Republican party in the South during the last quarter of the nineteenth century can be attributed in some measure to the efforts of its national leaders to win support in the region. In a period of extraordinarily close elections, Republican leaders, frequently of Whiggish background and usually conservative in their views, turned naturally enough to their counterparts in the South—to what one Republican politician referred to as "the same class of men in the South as are Republicans in the North"—in an endeavor to head off radical policies and perpetuate their control of the national government. Nor was it certain in the years immediately after Reconstruction that the Negro vote would steadily decline or that small white farmers and laborers would unanimously support the Democratic party.

Seeing the cleavages that divided southern Democrats and recognizing the bankruptcy of their own Reconstruction politics, Republicans approached the "southern question" in a growing mood of experimentation. President Hayes, dreaming of a strong Republican party in the South, sought to attract southern conservatives with a generous patronage policy and favorable legislation. As it became more evident that Southerners of Whiggish ancestry were finding a comfortable home in the Bourbon Democracy, James A. Garfield and Chester A. Arthur began to encourage independent movements that flickered across the southern skies as if marking the approach of a sectional storm. Benjamin Harrison attempted to use federal intervention, through the "force bill," to protect the voting rights of Negroes and whites in the South. And in the agrarian upheaval of the 1890's, Republican leaders tried to work out successful coalitions with Populists and dissident Democrats.

But success was limited. The most spectacular Republican efforts to perfect a coalition politics—in Virginia in the 1880's and North Carolina in the 1890's—provoked bitter conflict and recrimination, and in the long run diminished the party's strength in the region. These episodes also revealed the immensity of the obstacles confronting the Republicans. Their party lacked money, leaders, and newspapers in the South, and its ranks were torn by recurrent factionalism involving personal rivalry and conflict between "black and tan" and "lily-white" groups. "From nearly every Republican county convention," reported a Tennessee newspaper in 1900, "comes the same story: Two conventions, a split and contesting delegations to the state convention." Furthermore, southern whites could not remove from their minds the Reconstruction image of Republicanism and, despite the willingness of many Republican leaders to abandon their reliance upon Negro support, Southerners continued to associate the G.O.P. with fears of Negro domination. The Republicans also encountered fraud and intimidation, as well as discriminatory election machinery and state legislation designed to reduce their strength at the polls. Under such circumstances, it was virtually impossible to formulate a policy on the national level that would appeal to the enemies of the Bourbons in the South and at the same time satisfy powerful Republican interests outside the region. Thus the overtures Arthur made to the independents of a radical stripe in the South proved disquieting to orthodox Republicans. The change of sentiment in the North, reflecting the drift away from Reconstruction egalitarianism as well as the powerful influence of business elements in the Republican party, doomed Harrison's attempt to secure the passage of the "force bill." And to complicate matters even more, the very threat of such legislation became an effective weapon in the hands of those who championed white supremacy and the Solid South.

Had the Bourbon Democrats been confronted only with the Republican challenge, they might have retained a greater degree of equanimity. But almost from the beginning they were faced with intraparty dissension and the emergence of independent movements which held out the dreaded possibility of a merger with the Republicans and a transfer of political control. The frenzy of the efforts conservative Democrats made to solidify southern white men rose and fell in direct proportion to the waxing and waning of political independentism in the South.

One of the earliest of these movements, and the most significant before the Populist Revolt, was the Readjuster Movement in Virginia. This movement developed in the late 1870's when the state's politics was reshaped on the

basis of a contest between those who insisted upon fund-
ing Virginia's large debt and those who demanded its
"readjustment." The times were ripe for a political upheaval. The Republican party had been repudiated and
was badly disorganized, while the triumphant Bourbons
were faced with the problem of guiding an unwieldy
party and providing answers to a number of perplexing
questions, including the handling of the state debt. Economic conditions were poor, the people complained about
inequitable taxes, and the schools suffered from inadequate
support. Criticism of the conservative Democratic leadership increased, farmers began to see political implications
in the Granger movement, and some Virginians were
attracted to Greenbackism. A remarkable political messiah
now appeared on the scene to lead the democratic revolt.
His name was William Mahone, ex-Confederate general,
railroad builder, erstwhile conservative, and political
organizer extraordinary.

The movement which Mahone led reflected the geographic and social composition of Virginia. It appealed to
the small white farmers and the poorer classes, especially
in the western part of the state, and it succeeded in com-
bining these elements with a substantial number of
Negroes, most of whom lived in the lowlands of the eastern areas. The Readjuster leaders, characteristically, were
middle-class men on the make who found few opportunities for political distinction in the conservative regime of
the Bourbons. The Conservatives, as the Democrats were
wont to call themselves, had about them an aura of
aristocracy and Confederate mythology, but their fiscal
orthodoxy and their laissez-faire preachments brought
them powerful allies from the industrial-minded urban
centers.

The duration of Readjuster control was brief but the
movement greatly influenced Virginia politics. Capturing

control of the state legislature in 1879, the Readjusters soon dominated every branch of the Virginia government, including at one time the two United States Senate seats and six seats in the national House of Representatives. They readjusted the state debt, revised the system of taxation, repealed the poll tax, abolished the whipping post, provided liberal appropriations for education, and enacted legislation favorable to labor. At the same time, under Mahone's leadership, a patronage machine was created and an attempt was made to combine with the Republicans. The Conservatives, meanwhile, took advantage of Readjuster mistakes and raised the cry of Republican control and Negro domination. By the mid-eighties they had redeemed the state from Mahoneism. But in the process they borrowed some of the democratic features of the Readjuster program and, like many southern Democrats in the nineties, sought to broaden their appeal to the less-privileged elements in the white population.

Although Virginia was the only southern state in which independents wrested control from the Bourbons in the 1880's, almost all of the former Confederate states experienced some degree of independent revolt in the decade following Reconstruction. Some of this political independence represented conflict over state debts and fiscal policies similar to the controversy in Virginia. While the repudiation or readjustment of Reconstruction debts was generally popular in the South and inextricably connected with the overthrow of Radical rule, it is significant that the "State-Credit" attitude of the Whig-industrial elements was a powerful influence in the Bourbon Democracy. On the other hand, there was a close kinship between the readjusters and repudiationists and the political independents who espoused inflationary proposals and other economic ideas with a radical tinge. The opposition to the Democratic conservatives frequently developed over such local issues as the unequal division of educational funds, inequitable tax rates, business favoritism, the malodorous operation of the convict lease system, and local-option elections, but in every state there were charges of machine politics, "ring" rule, and manipulated elections. There was also dissatisfaction with the malapportionment of state legislatures and the black belts' use of Negro votes to strengthen their position. The convention system of making nominations and choosing party leaders, moreover, was often linked to the system of representation, which meant that black counties were given delegates far out of proportion to their voting strength. In South Carolina, to cite one example given by C. Vann Woodward, "the upland plebeians found they had redeemed the state from the Carpetbaggers only to lose it to the lowland bosses."

Independentism was a real force in the South of the seventies and eighties. In Georgia an independent movement elected William H. Felton and Emory L. Speer to Congress, but failed in an effort to overturn the Bourbon control of the state. In 1878 William M. Lowe was elected to Congress as an independent from a north Alabama district, and in the same year a Greenback-Labor candidate in Texas won a congressional seat. The Greenbackers made a strong showing in gubernatorial contests in Kentucky, Alabama, and Arkansas during the next two years, and during the early eighties Democratic politicians reflecting the economic radicalism of Greenbackism challenged the conservative political control in South Carolina, Mississippi, Texas, and other states. While the Greenback movement failed to obtain a substantial number of votes in most southern states, like other independent movements of the period it mirrored strong dissatisfaction with Bourbon authority and socio-economic cleavages in southern society that belied the claim of a Solid South.

Yet by the mid-eighties the edge of independentism in most southern states seemed to have been blunted. All of the old techniques of social and economic pressure perfected in the battles against the Reconstruction Radicals had been employed in ruthless campaigns against party independents and insurgents. The same methods would be applied even more savagely against the Populists. At the same time, economic conditions improved a bit; farm commodity prices increased somewhat as the nation entered into an era of unprecedented railroad construction and experienced a mighty industrial expansion. There was a feeling of general satisfaction in the South, moreover, with Grover Cleveland's victory in 1884 and the return of the Democrats to national power early the next year. But the relatively placid years of the mid-eighties were not to last long, and the late 1880's and much of the decade of the nineties witnessed growing agrarian distress, industrial crisis, and political conflict all over the country.

What historians call the "agrarian revolt" was not peculiar to the South—it was also a western phenomenon—but its effect upon southern politics can scarcely be overemphasized. The movement was a long time coming to a head; it gathered strength, in the South at least, from most of the independent movements and other expressions of agrarian radicalism that littered the landscape of the 1870's and 1880's. Although the farmers' revolt grew out of a long and pervasive period of agricultural depression, at its fundamental level it was a protest and a countermovement against the encroachment of modern industrialism upon rural society and values. The agrarian grievances possessed a solid core of reality. Farmers in the South and West for two and a half decades after 1870 suffered from steadily declining agricultural prices, inequitable taxes, inadequate credit facilities and high interest charges, a contracting currency, a high tariff on the products they bought, and monopolistic power in business, whether exercised by the middle men they dealt with at first hand or the powerful railroads and industrial "trusts," somewhat further removed. Furthermore, during these years farmers frequently experienced a social stagnation and loss of personal dignity and community status that produced widespread despair, resentment, and defiance in the agricultural regions. In the South the situation facing the farmer, especially the millions of small operators and tenants, was even worse since it reflected the post-bellum revolution that introduced peculiar and repressive arrangements in labor, land tenure, and credit.

The manner in which southern farmers were driven to organize in their attempts to counter the injurious effects of the postwar agricultural institutions and the new industrialism can be seen in the numerous farm organizations that sprang up in the 1880's. Some of these groups reflected the interest of small farmers and dispossessed agrarian elements in radical economic schemes, while others were oriented toward the more conservative and capitalistic views of large planters, lumbermen, and the like. But both types found a home in the Farmers' Alliance, an organization that came sweeping out of the Southwest in the late 1880's, pulling other farm groups and thousands of unaffiliated farmers into its ranks. It was the Southern Alliance, as it was called, that synthesized a platform and a philosophy out of the inchoate materials tossed up by agricultural depression and defiance. It was the Southern Alliance, as Theodore Saloutos has demonstrated in his careful study of farmer movements in the South, that produced the economic and political ideas that were given national currency by the People's party. The Alliance,

Professor Saloutos concludes, was perhaps the single most important liberalizing force the South nourished during the late nineteenth century.

By 1890 the Alliance movement had become an important political factor in the South and the West. It sponsored a host of reform measures looking to currency inflation, government-based credit, land reform, railroad and trust regulation, and the democratization of the political process. The complicated story of the agrarian revolt that followed in the South has been brilliantly told by Professor Woodward in a general work and closely analyzed by other scholars in detailed monographs. We need only to suggest the pattern the movement wove into the fabric of southern politics. In the beginning the agrarian radicals tried to capture the Democratic party in the South, and in the elections of 1890 they seemed to carry all before them by winning notable victories for the Alliance standard in several states. They could point to victories in more than half the legislative seats in eight states, to six Alliance governors, and to more than fifty congressmen bearing the organization's stamp of approval. But it proved more difficult to secure legislative reforms than to obtain campaign endorsements from Democratic politicians, and by 1892 the formation of the Populist party on a national basis injected the "third party" issue into southern politics.

The result was incomparably bitter and confusing. Many southern farmers took the plunge and became members of the new party, while others who subscribed to Populist principles attempted to avoid the pain of breaking ancient party loyalties by calling themselves "Jeffersonian Democrats" and the like. Most Southerners, however, remained loyal to the Democratic party, responding to the Cleveland campaign, the wild talk about the "force bill," and the approval of Alliance demands by some Democratic

leaders. Even so, the People's party showed surprising
strength in many southern states. When the Cleveland
administration foundered amidst the currents of depression and economic chaos, while demonstrating its conservative orthodoxy and lack of understanding of agrarian
unrest, southern Populists looked ahead to greater things.
The elections of 1894 gave them a good deal of encouragement, for the third party made gains in several southern
states. It did particularly well in North Carolina, Alabama,
and Georgia, receiving almost 45 per cent of the state election ballots in the last state. In North Carolina the Democrats lost both houses of the legislature to the Populists
and Republicans, who then prepared the ground for the
ill-fated fusionist regime that captured control of the
entire state in 1896. Meanwhile, the new party attempted
to fuse with the Republicans on the state and local levels
in several other states.

The denouement came with the election of 1896. By
that time the opposition to Cleveland had captured the
Democratic party in virtually every southern state and, to
the consternation of the Populists, took over a large part
of the Populist platform, including the irridescent free
silver symbol. The southern Democrats then helped
place William Jennings Bryan at the head of their party's
national ticket. The ever-present danger that the third
party would join forces with the Republicans in the South,
as it did so spectacularly in North Carolina, was a factor of
great consequence in this liberalization of the southern
Democracy. For while it guaranteed the perpetuation of
Democratic supremacy in the South, it did so by keeping
within its folds such leaders as Benjamin R. Tillman and
James S. Hogg. The fact that such agrarian reformers
would not make common cause with the Populists was
surely one reason for the latter's failure. Meanwhile, the
dilemma of the Populists, especially those in the South,

was as cruel as it was baffling. There was, in fact, no way out for the People's party. It could not resist the pressure to endorse Bryan, and the fusion—and confusion—that followed the Nebraskan's valiant campaign brought the virtual collapse of the third party everywhere.

The importance of the Populist movement in the history of southern politics is not always appreciated. "In retrospect," wrote William W. Ball in 1911, "the artificiality of the differences of the nineties is plain, and . . . they did not permanently divide the people." The flurry caused by the agrarian radicals soon passed and "the people took up again their accustomed modes of thinking and doing. Though the division of the people was sharp and accompanied with cruel laceration, it was not deep—it was only skin deep." This interpretation scarcely does justice to the facts. William Garrott Brown was more perceptive. "I call that particular change a revolution," he wrote, "and I would use a stronger term if there were one; for no other political movement—not that of 1776, nor that of 1860-1861—ever altered Southern life so profoundly."

The southern farmers, like numerous other economic and social elements in the United States during this era, had tried with some success to consolidate their forces to meet the threat of powerful interests and competing groups being welded together by the new industrialism. Much of the radicalism associated with Populism was indigenous to the South. The movement probably had its greatest strength in that region, and it is altogether likely that but for the presence of the Negro the Populists would have gained political control in several southern states. It is true that there was a decided provincialism and negativism involved in Populistic philosophy. One historian has characterized the Southern Alliance (which first formulated the Populist program) as "pro-agricultural, anti-urban, anti-merchant, anti-banker, anti-foreign," while

Senator John Sharp Williams described the operative
motive in Populism as "a revolt against all manner of
superiorities."

Yet the Populists were primarily responsible for a widespread revival of Jeffersonian and Jacksonian principles—
and for the extension of those principles. Their espousal
of positive governmental action, business control, and
political democracy became a vital part of the democratic
tradition in the South and the nation. By their emphasis
on monetary inflation and credit needs, marketing reforms,
minimum prices and acreage controls, and better farming
methods, southern farmer movements in the late nineteenth century gave a heritage to the twentieth century of
great economic and political importance.

The Populist upheaval enormously invigorated politics
in the South. Suddenly there were contests for state and
local positions that had real meaning—with party choices
and clear-cut issues. The social conflict that attended political controversies in the nineties was intense and often
bitter; it reflected the fundamental basis of the democracy
that was continually struggling to assert itself in the region.
For the Populist movement challenged the "New South"
system frontally, challenged the southern mythology that
helped support it, challenged its conservative policies and
its political oligarchies. Populism threatened a combination of the dispossessed farmers and Negroes along economic and social lines and on the basis of economic and
political action. It brought into sharp relief long-time
cleavages which the Redeemers had never been able completely to suppress.

The rank-and-file agrarian radicals came from the lower
social and economic classes. They disliked the political
domination of the black belts and the powerful alliances
between plantation leaders and city politicians that usually
controlled the state governments. They were revolting not

only against conditions that shackled them to a colonial
economy but also against a local political system that
denied them an effective voice in political affairs. It was, as
the saying went, a struggle of the "wool-hat boys" against
the "silk-hat bosses." There may have been a few "silk-
hatted" Populists—certainly there were some well-to-do
farmers in the movement—and we should not make the
mistake of interpreting Populism primarily in terms of
class. Yet, in the South at least, social and economic divisions were clearly revealed during the controversies over
Populism, and they rested on far more than the demands
for agricultural parity.

The fury of the rebellion was strong enough to force
concessions from the Bourbon regimes in most of the
southern states. But the Solid South remained. What happened in the 1890's was not unlike what happened in
1860-61. In both of these great political crises in the South,
the black belts succeeded in overcoming those who opposed their policies and in using the threats to their control as a means of coercing future solidarity. Democratic
leaders in the nineties hurriedly invoked the race issue,
rang the changes on the dangers of bolting the party, and
fell back on skillful election maneuvers and tricks to win
threatened districts. "Any Democrat might just as well go
straight into the Republican party as into the ranks of its
active ally, the People's party," warned a prominent Democratic newspaper in Tennessee. The conservatives never
tired of pointing to the fusionist government of North
Carolina and pleading for redemption from the horrors of
a second Reconstruction. The Populists in the South, observes Vann Woodward, "daily faced the implacable dog-
mas of racism, white solidarity, white supremacy, and the
bloody shirt." Small wonder that southern whites should
learn, as a perceptive contemporary put it, to set men
above political principles and "good government" above

freedom of thought. Some Southerners, of course, were affected by the constitutional arguments and state-rights fetishism of the conservatives; they were suspicious of the centralizing effect of Populist remedies or feared new competition and injurious regulation of local business interests.

The traumatic experience of the 1890's also demonstrated how even the more democratic currents in a region so powerfully affected by tradition and racist mythology could be turned into reactionary channels. For one of the most immediate and tragic results of the Populist movement was the stimulus it gave to Negro disfranchisement. Both the conservatives and the radicals agreed that the political corruption of the 1890's was demoralizing and must be ended. The conservatives were deeply shocked by the possibility of a political alliance between the humbler whites and the Negroes on the basis of common economic interests. The radicals, bitterly contending that Negro votes had been used by their opponents to defeat them, abandoned their fair play principles of the early nineties and turned on the colored man. The fierce internal struggles within the party of Redemption, going back to the 1880's, persuaded many people to advocate Negro disfranchisement. In some states white farmers, eager to throw off the black-belt domination based in part on Negro votes, took the lead in calling for constitutional changes. Yet the poorer whites, who inhabited the mountain and hill regions in large numbers, looked with suspicion upon disfranchisement proposals which might be turned in their own direction.

In the end the restrictionists carried the day, though not without a fight, and the long-range effect of the measures they pushed through disfranchised not only the great majority of the Negroes but many white men as well. Contemporary white Southerners were inclined to view the suffrage restrictions as a necessary step, even a reform, but the race question could not be so easily exorcised. It supplied the politician with an issue that aroused the average white man even more powerfully than economic and class exhortations.

In withstanding the assaults of the Populists the Solid South had become institutionalized. The guardians of sectional solidarity had had little cause for complacency during the two decades prior to 1896: the People's party was only the last and most serious in a long series of running battles with party rebels, third parties, and Republicans. But the dikes held during the mighty storm of the nineties, which left in its wake the wreckage of the third-party dreams, bitter disillusionment in the minds of many men, and a general yearning for an end to such internecine struggles. A man would think long and hard before leaving the southern Democracy in the future. The frustrations of the 1890's were almost more than some men could bear, and in their subsequent careers many of them followed the pattern Richard Hofstadter has called the "deconversion from reform to reaction." Not all Southerners, however, were embittered and without hope. The events of the nineties were not without their positive effects, and many reform-minded Democrats were exhilarated by the changes taking place in southern politics. They looked ahead to the day when the promises of the agrarian reform movements would become a reality. The meaning of these varied reactions for the future was simply this: if the climactic events of the nineties ushered in a generation of unswerving loyalty to the Democratic party on the part of Southerners, they also pointed the way to important developments of a "democratic" nature within the one-party system.

LECTURE

THREE

The One-Party South in Mid-Passage

FOLLOWING THE POPULIST UPHEAVAL THE SUPREMACY OF the Democratic party in the South became complete. The Republican party in most of the southern states declined to insignificant proportions, a skeleton party racked by factionalism and perpetuated only by the desire of its leaders for federal offices and their quadrennial role in the national conventions. There was no Republican party in the South, admitted Theodore Roosevelt in 1901: there was "simply a set of black and white scalawags." No new third party appeared to take the place of the Populists. The gathering shadows of Negro disfranchisement had fallen over the region and in the public mind the formal political proscription of the race assumed a character so widely accepted and so elemental in its "rightness" as to make it seem almost God-given and eternal. Farmers with special interests and sharply-felt grievances there were— and also men of independent mind and class hostility—but they had learned well, too well in fact, the lessons taught in the school of Populism and third-party radicalism. Henceforth they would take pains to abide steadfastly in the Democratic house of their youth. Now and then, of course, a keen observer might note significant implications in the economic and social changes taking place in the sunnier years after the turn of the century, but such changes were subtle in their political manifestation, promising at most important alterations in a time too distant to disturb the regularity of a people's thought.

The hopelessness of southern Republicanism quickly became apparent in the years after 1900. Momentarily, it is true, there was talk of a Republican revival in the South. The growing capitalist sentiment in the region encouraged a certain restlessness among businessmen and expressions of dissatisfaction with the Democratic party's position on such issues as the tariff, ship subsidies, and foreign policy. Many Southerners responded favorably to Theodore Roosevelt's leadership and, despite his affronts to their racial sensibilities, he aroused a good deal of enthusiasm below the Potomac. But he received few southern votes. William Howard Taft, whose policies appealed to many southern Democrats unhappy with the Bryanization of their party, showed considerable strength in several southern states in the election of 1908, but his efforts to attract a conservative following in the South proved unavailing and were swallowed up in the disruption of his administration and the revival of the Democratic party on the national level.

Nevertheless, Republicanism in the border states during this period had become ascendant, giving this area a strong two-party system. The Republican party also remained of some consequence in Virginia, North Carolina, and Tennessee: in each of these states the Republicans normally elected one or two congressmen and controlled the local governments in substantial parts of the mountain country. But it was hard to be a practicing Republican in most sections of the South. As the Republican governor of North Carolina confessed in 1898, "the irritations incident to being a Republican and living in the South, are getting to be too rank to be borne. . . ."

The Solid South was real enough in terms of the region's Democratic loyalties. Yet, strangely enough, the South soon entered upon an era of almost unparalleled intraparty competition. It was almost as if the predictions that disfranchisement would enable white Southerners to divide in a meaningful way over genuine issues were coming to pass. But the real reasons for these political struggles were only indirectly, if at all, related to the politics of race, which in any event continued to preoccupy many southern politicians. It should not be assumed that this bifactionalism gave the region a substitute for the two-party system. The extent and significance of such cleavages have varied from state to state and from time to time, always subject to the vagaries of the amorphous and highly personalized politics resulting from the dominance of a single party. Nevertheless, an extraordinary amount of competition has existed in the politics of the New South, and this competition has usually reflected the historic divisions and the changing character of southern society.

While there is reason to believe that a genuine two-party system is superior to a uniparty politics, it is not altogether clear just what the relationship is between party politics and the actual operation of the government. Nor is it plain what difference, if any, is to be found between the way the power structure of a community influences the political process in a one-party state and the way it affects politics in a two-party system. At any rate, recent comparative studies of state politics in the United States suggest that the competition, and perhaps the democracy, of certain one-party states is as great as in that of some more bi-partisan commonwealths.

One thing that quickened the spirit of southern politics during the early years of the twentieth century was the continuing revolt of the farmers. Although they abandoned independent political action and concentrated upon means of increasing farm efficiency and productivity, the farmers continued to serve as a strong liberalizing force in southern politics. Their organizations, institutes, and journals agitated for better methods of cultivation, voluntary crop withholding and acreage reduction schemes, and a host of other co-operative ventures. The Farmers' Union, the foremost agricultural organization in the region, kept alive much of the radicalism of the Farmers' Alliance, which it resembled in many ways, and sought to meet the needs of small farmers and sharecroppers. The anti-monopoly sentiment that infused southern politics during this period owed most perhaps to the rural elements which were attempting through their own organizations to defend themselves in the market place against the operation of the cotton exchanges and such powerful combinations as the American Tobacco Company. On occasion these agrarian revolts led to outright war, as in the tobacco regions of Kentucky and Tennessee. They also account for the outbreak of rural Socialism in Oklahoma, Louisiana, and one or two other states in the years just prior to World War I.

But in general the political activities of southern farmers in the early twentieth century followed less radical paths. The farm groups became an important force in the broader movements to regulate railroad rates, insurance and banking practices, and public utility companies, and to restrict the influence of such corporations in politics. They lent their support to the good roads movement, to the public education campaigns, and to the reformation of party organization and election machinery on the state and local levels. They were instrumental in the passage of congressional legislation to create a parcel post system and a bureau of marketing in the United States Department of Agriculture. The farmers' movement really came into its own during the Wilson administration, when many of the agrarian demands were incorporated into reforms dealing with the tariff, banking and currency legislation, and anti-trust policy, and their particular interests were reflected in a comprehensive farm credit system, an agricultural extension program, and various other measures.

The growing strength of the farmers' movement in the years after 1900 and the influence it exerted in southern politics suggest another, more general development that grew out of the upheaval of the nineties. This was the way in which Populism and Bryanism contributed to the formation of liberal-conservative election alliances and party factions. Populism, as one scholar has remarked, left a habit of radicalism in the upland areas of the South. Few leaders have been more popular among rank-and-file Southerners than William Jennings Bryan, and Populist principles survived to leaven the factional politics of the South during the twentieth century. Bryan's leadership and the democratic program associated with it greatly strengthened the liberal wing of the Democratic party that challenged the conservative faction year after year in virtually every southern state. "In the South," declared one liberal leader of this era, "we vainly fancy that we have only a Democratic party. Both parties are in fact fully developed among us, all claiming the same name and fighting out their battles under the party organization."

However exaggerated such illusions might have been, there is no denying the existence of fairly clear-cut divi-sions along liberal-conservative lines during the first decade and a half of the twentieth century. The conservatives, representing in general the old black-belt hegemony, had managed as a rule to ride out the storm of the nineties without losing control of party machinery and state governments, and with a minimum of concessions to the agrarian radicals within the Democratic party. But now they faced new threats and, as it proved, a more subtle and comprehensive challenge to their continued domination. Since the conservatives exerted disproportionate power in the political system, they fought the liberals on the highly practical basis of the "ins" versus the "outs." But their opposition was grounded in socio-economic conflicts and ideological differences.

The powerful and well-to-do, whether representing agrarian or commercial and industrial interests, abhorred Bryanism, with its promise of business regulation, social reform, and political democracy. Such a man, for instance, as James Calvin Hemphill, the conservative editor of the Charleston *News and Courier,* considered Bryan a radical ne'er-do-well. Hemphill was a votary of the capitalist spirit in the South. His views accorded almost perfectly with those of William Howard Taft, and he denounced the direct primary, Tillmanism, prohibition, and the centralization taking place in the American political system. Many times during the next few years men like Hemphill were inclined to throw up their hands and admit that the country "is gone hell bent." Or as another South Carolina conservative exclaimed in 1912, " 'Yer Dimocracy,' as Carlyle called it, is a good deal of a delusion and much of a disgust."

An important factor in the rise of this democracy and in the intraparty competition in the South was the widespread adoption during the early part of the century of the direct primary and the liberalization of the election machinery insofar as white participation was concerned.

It is true that the white primary became the final and most absolute of the many barriers blocking the road of southern Negroes to any effective involvement in the region's political affairs. But it is also true that the device was adopted in some states not so much as a disfranchising measure (Negroes had already lost their political rights in most instances) as a means of introducing a greater degree of popular government.

Black-belt and conservative domination rested in no small part on the convention system of making nominations and the centralized control of party machinery. This encouraged the formation of "cliques" and "machines" that perpetuated themselves through careful use of patronage, alliances with influential business interests, and a philosophy of laissez faire. Dissatisfaction with such oligarchical control had done much to inspire the independent movements of the 1880's and the agrarian radicals of the 1890's. These old grievances were reinforced by Bryan's politics and the growing popularity of "direct democracy" in various parts of the country. In the South the democratization of the political process also owed something to the concessions the regular Democrats were forced to make to maintain the Solid South and to the searching examination of party machinery and campaign practices made in the campaigns for disfranchisement. On paper, at least, the conservatives were persuaded to acknowledge the desirability of an extension of white democracy. At any rate, most southern states soon adopted the primary system and attempted to control campaign practices by legislation. In some states this revolutionized politics and in all of them it contributed to the emergence of the liberal-conservative factionalism referred to above.

It also contributed to what Roger W. Shugg has called the "uprising of the poor whites." During Populist days leaders like Tom Watson and Ben Tillman ignited the spark of political consciousness among common white men, and when the direct primary came into widespread use shortly thereafter, partly in response to their demands, these little men awoke to the realization that they possessed a new political power and that politicians were beginning to court their affections.

The most notable example of "the revolt of the red-necks" took place in Mississippi. Building upon geographic and class conflicts endemic in Mississippi and upon the Populist hostility toward business corporations (particularly the large lumber interests and insurance companies), the reformers took advantage of the state-wide primary system introduced in 1902 to elect James K. Vardaman to the governorship in 1903. Vardaman and Theodore G. Bilbo, who succeeded "the Great White Chief" as the champion of the common man in Mississippi, revolutionized the state's politics by enlisting the support of the poorer whites of the hill regions and the piney woods. "You can look at the back of my neck and see that I am a Vardaman man," declared a Mississippian in 1910. Despite the fact that the poll tax and other disqualifying clauses adopted in connection with Negro disfranchisement prevented many of the submerged elements from voting, the "rednecks" were still able to seize control of the state government from the delta planters and their business allies. They proceeded to dominate the state's political affairs for almost two decades after 1903.

A large part of Vardaman's appeal stemmed from his inflammatory use of the race question, but he and Bilbo also attacked the rich and played upon class conflict. Both men made themselves the main issue. Yet the whole hardly equals the sum of the parts. In many ways Vardaman and Bilbo proved to be good governors. They secured the enactment of penal reforms, railroad and utility regulation, an important tax equalization system, and greater support for public education and state institutions. However prejudiced or misdirected their campaigns may have been, they were responsible for a new social and political awareness, even a class consciousness, on the part of the masses of white Mississippians. They energized the state's politics and forced aspiring politicians to go to the people.

The result of this democratization of the white South was often salutary, but not always so. "Men of the people" like Vardaman and Coleman L. Blease of South Carolina proclaimed their faith in the power and wisdom of the masses and began to give expression to the social grievances —and to the prejudices and passions—of the "rednecks" and the "wool hat boys" whose number was legion in the early twentieth-century South. The demagogues pictured themselves as men of action who would attack the rich, destroy the trusts, and keep "the nigger in his place." According to Wilbur J. Cash, Tillman brought forth the "whole bold, dashing, hell-of-a-fellow complex precisely in terms of the generality themselves," while Blease exemplified "the whole tradition of extravagance, of sectionalism and Negrophobia in Southern politics." Blease, wrote Ludwig Lewisohn, was "the typical leader of the democracy of the New South—ostentatiously large wool hat, dark rather fierce eyes, heavy black mustache, gaudy insignia on a heavy watch-chain, a man who radiated or wanted to radiate a constant ferocity against the irreligious, the impure, 'Nigger-lovers,' aristocrats, 'pap-suckers,' Yankees, intellectuals, a son of the soil and of the mob with a chip on his shoulder."

The excesses and irrelevancies of such leaders were perhaps a measure of the difficulties they faced in attempting to break the political domination of the vested interests, especially in the lower South. The tragedy in the leadership of many of these men—aside from their resort to racist exhortations—was that, once elected, they usually became less rebellious, less representative of the poorer classes, often making their peace with the political hierarchies and the business interests they had recently denounced and threatened. Fundamentally, the fault probably lay in a serious social malady. There seems to be a correlation between the bankruptcy of leadership in the case of some of these politicians and the mounting scourge of farm tenancy. The lack of an urban-based liberalism also contributed to the frustration of their reform proposals and to the triumph of conservative planters and business interests. Even so, these "men of the people" did much to give politics in the South whatever form and coherence it possessed; they evoked a fierce loyalty from their supporters, and most of them served at least a cathartic function by acting as a "safety valve for discontent."

One of the most important rallying points in the reform politics of the South during the progressive era was the anti-corporation movement. For a quarter of a century before World War I Southern politics rang with the verbal blows of the battle to control powerful corporations. The railroads were the focal point of the anti-corporation attack, for they were a political force to be reckoned with throughout the region, and in some states their dictates were the most influential consideration in legislative and administrative action. Their liberal use of lucrative retainers, highly-paid lobbyists, subsidized newspapers, and free passes, not to mention their high rates and discriminatory freight charges, made them the natural enemy of reformers everywhere. Indeed, the first coalescence of progressives in several southern states came with movements for railroad regulation and rate reductions, notably in Georgia, Alabama, North Carolina, and Texas.

Much of this anti-trust sentiment was carried over from

Populism, being kept alive by farm organizations and journals as well as by the rhetoric of politicians in rural areas who attacked the cotton exchanges and the trusts. But the rural agitation against the railroads and big business was vastly strengthened by the support of many urban elements, especially freight bureaus, chambers of commerce, and other groups interested more in the competitive advantage of lower rates or preferential treatment than any all-out assault on large corporations. Thus the railroad regulatory movement in the South represented the response of the region to significant economic and social changes occurring within its borders, changes that were slowly diversifying its economy and differentiating its people. Yet it should be noted that both farmers and city dwellers resented the colonial status of the South's industry and commerce, and this resentment helped give a strong sectional cast to southern progressivism.

While the agrarian elements supplied much of the anti-corporation radicalism that permeated southern politics and gave support to many of the reform movements of the progressive period, it was the urban communities that sparked the region's progressivism and provided much of its leadership. Economic progress, too limited to alter the social structure of the region very much during the postwar generation, was beginning to have its effect. Economic and social advances in North Carolina, for instance, encouraged the development of a new urban liberalism, an educational renaissance, and more responsible state and local government.

Middle-class and professional values were making themselves felt in many parts of the South, businessmen were beginning to enlist in the ranks of the reformers, and the editors of liberal newspapers like the Atlanta *Journal,* the Columbia *State,* and the Raleigh *News and Observer* were becoming powerful instruments in the fight for progressive measures. In the towns and cities especially there was a tendency to see the South through new and more critical eyes, and a yearning to see it participate in the national reforms. A group of women reformers began to emerge in every state, organizing for their own emancipation and for the amelioration of various social evils. Middle-class, moderate, and hopeful, the southern progressives read in the signs of the time the approach of a new day for the South. "The old moss-backs will soon be gone, thank the Lord," declared an Atlanta minister in 1908. "Here, then, will come a generation of young men and women to be transformed by the quickening forces of a new environment."

Although the conditions that moved the southern progressives to action were often represented in the national press as peculiar to the "backward South," they were in fact fundamentally the same conditions that accompanied the industrialization of other parts of the country. Nor was the response of southern reformers to the evils and abuses of industrialization and urbanization very different from that of other American reformers in this period. They showed a growing awareness of the need for governmental intervention to deal with pressing social problems. Such issues as public utility regulation, public education campaigns, child-labor legislation, penal reform, factory regulation, municipal reorganization, and the improvement of the mechanisms of representative government appealed to the practical self-interest and the humanitarianism of many urban men and women. There was also a strong interest among farmers and city folk alike in "moral" legislation to control such evils as the liquor traffic and gambling.

Political reformers arose in every state in the South to take advantage of this reform sentiment. Some of these men were demagogues and some were conservatives masquerading as progressives. Others were genuine liberals, ranging in type from moderate humanitarians, concerned about such things as penal reform and public education, to agrarian radicals who talked like Populists. In evaluating the liberalizing factors in southern politics during the first two decades of the twentieth century, one must not overlook the important role played by these leaders. Although the dangers and limitations of a highly personalized leadership were undoubtedly very great in a one-party system, it was impossible in such a system to challenge the status quo without a powerful individual to lead the movement. Only a strong leader could arouse sufficient enthusiasm among the voters to overcome the natural advantage of the conservatives in dominating politics and government at the state and local levels. Only a bold and resourceful politician could bring together into a popular coalition such disparate elements as farmers, urban workers, middle-class professionals, and businessmen. It should be pointed out in this connection that, while obeisance was made to the principle of separation of powers by those who thought about such constitutional niceties, the public increasingly came to regard the governor as a legislative leader and to hold him responsible for formulating a legislative program.

In some southern states that experienced substantial reform, such as North Carolina and Texas, there were several important liberal leaders. In others one man and his administration as governor gave the major impetus to a reform movement and sometimes came to symbolize the whole movement. This was largely true, for example, in the case of Andrew Montague in Virginia, Hoke Smith in Georgia, Napoleon B. Broward in Florida, and Braxton B. Comer in Alabama. In Tennessee a peculiar and possibly a revealing political drama unfolded. The split between the liberal and regular Democrats became so pronounced that the liberal wing of the party fused with the Republicans. This remarkable combination elected a liberal Republican named Benjamin W. Hooper to the governorship in 1910 and 1912, and his administration produced some significant reforms in the progressive tradition.

Whatever their limitations, the more effective of the southern progressives did much to encourage a widespread bifactionalism in the Democratic party and to present the voters in the primaries with a real choice between conservative and liberal candidates. Southern progressives added a good deal to the functions of government and secured a substantial body of reforms, but their success varied from state to state and they neglected some fundamental problems, including the increase of farm tenancy and the worsening plight of the more depressed farm classes. Southern progressivism was for "whites only" and some of the progressives could not refrain from invoking the race question in their political contests.

The progressive leaders learned, just as they did in other parts of the country, that it was one thing to win elections and quite another to secure the passage of progressive legislation. They also discovered that even after reforms were adopted they often failed the test of administrative effectiveness. There were still other barriers to reform. The liberal factions generated by the progressive movement in the South had to pay the heavy cost of too-great reliance on personal politics. In order to be successful they must have powerful and colorful leaders, but when they were successful the leaders often loomed larger in the minds of the people than the reforms they advocated. Even more important was the inability of strong progressives to pass on their leadership to equally effective successors. There was no system to recruit and train leaders and no sure restraints in such an amorphous politics that would preserve discipline and coherence for any length of time.

Southern conservatives, observed Douglas S. Freeman a few years later, had "a disconcerting way of conquering their conquerors." They took advantage of spurious issues which seemed to turn up at the most inopportune moment for the progressives. Prohibition, for instance, diverted the liberal movement in some southern states. It tended to become the *raison d'être* of the reform movement, smoothing over the more natural patterns of conflict in the body politic and shifting attention from more pressing economic and social problems. The growing rural-urban cleavage also redounded to the advantage of those who sought to prevent the passage of liberal legislation. Farmers frequently felt that their interests were being neglected in the drive for commercial and industrial progress, and men like Tom Watson, in V. O. Key's phrase, "turned the towns into whipping boys." Economic reforms almost always encountered fierce opposition, and the South's social conservatism tempted both the opponents of reforms and politicians seeking votes and popular unity to appeal to issues of race and religion. After all, as T. Harry Williams has noted, "the mystique of unity" had become a force in itself—almost a third legend to go along with the Lost Cause and the Old South. There was still a powerful strain of the romantic and the irrelevant in southern politics. As John Andrew Rice wrote of his uncle, that inimitable South Carolina politician, "Cotton Ed" Smith, "At some point in every speech the Lord's will got mixed up with the boys in grey storming an impregnable height, the purity of Southern womanhood, Yankees, the glorious past and the still more glorious future, including the white man's sacred right to lynch. It was all very vague and inspiring."

The nomination and election of Woodrow Wilson, the

first southern-born President since Andrew Johnson, was both a reflection of and a contribution to southern progressivism. During the years 1911-1912 the movement to nominate Wilson, who was then achieving an impressive national reputation as a progressive governor of New Jersey, received the enthusiastic support of the liberal faction of the Democratic party in almost every southern state. The Wilson movement in the South, as Arthur S. Link has shown, was fundamentally a struggle for "progressive Democracy," a climactic conflict that was rooted in long-time divisions. It brought to the fore important issues that needed attention and provoked a great amount of interest in popular government and progressive reform. The Wilson movement served to give the liberal factions— some of which had been thwarted on the state level—a kind of national base and momentarily to sharpen the bifactional politics that had been developing in the South. Wilson's election also gave a new note of pride and satisfaction to millions of Southerners who could scarcely believe that a Southerner had won the highest office in the land. "Long ago I had despaired of ever seeing a man of Southern birth President," exclaimed a North Carolina judge, who felt that Wilson's election marked "an era in our national life. With it we have the ascendancy of men of Southern birth and residence to the seats of power and responsibility such as has never been seen in our day . . . . The world is looking on to witness the result."

Five members of Wilson's cabinet were born in the South and southern congressional leaders assumed a prominent role in the enactment of the extensive domestic reforms that the Wilson administration pressed in the years 1913-1917. A significant feature of the Wilson period was the preponderant control of congressional committee chairmanships by Southerners, whose seniority in service, growing out of the one-party system's operation, gave them precedence over non-southern Democrats in Congress. Another aspect of the South's relationship to Wilson's New Freedom was the influence of several neo-Populist congressmen from such states as Arkansas and Texas in forcing the administration to sponsor more radical agricultural, banking, and anti-trust legislation than Wilson had at first recommended. With the shift of interest from domestic matters to foreign problems, the South firmly upheld Wilson's diplomatic course, although some dissatisfaction existed in the cotton belt in 1914-1915, because of the administration's failure to adopt stronger measures to keep open the commercial routes to Continental Europe. After the war came, Southerners strongly supported it and they were equally staunch in their adherence to the President's peace proposals.

Yet the Wilson administration was ambivalent in its approach to the southern progressives. If Wilson appealed most strongly during the long pre-convention fight to the liberal wing of the southern Democracy and as President brought the enactment of a major part of the progressive program, the liberals south of the Potomac were nevertheless virtually immolated by the practical politics of the Wilson administration. As the leader of the Democratic party, Wilson was under great pressure to work for party unity. As a liberal President with a moderately progressive program, he could not afford to offend powerful congressional leaders and committee chairmen from the South, many of whom were not noted for their liberalism, and still hope to enact even the more important parts of his legislative program. The result was that, however unwillingly, the President and his lieutenants co-operated with those Southerners who were in power and, more often than not, failed to give much tangible aid to the liberal groups which had looked upon the Wilson movement as a means of overthrowing their conservative opponents on the state level. There were liberal protests in 1913 and 1914 throughout the South because the new administration's patronage policies were strengthening the control of conservative factions. This from an "original" Wilson leader in the South is typical: "The men who fought for Wilson, not because of his personality only or chiefly, but because he stood for what they believed in, have been ostracized by him." Perhaps Wilson could do nothing else. At any rate, he could take some satisfaction from the steady support given him by many southern conservatives, who proved amenable to the blandishments of federal patronage and the traditions of party regularity.

There was still another factor that tended to inhibit the fullest expression of Wilsonian liberalism in the South. This was the restraining hand laid upon southern politicians by the growing influence of the region's industrial promoters. The textile interests in the Carolinas and Georgia, the iron and steel manufacturers in Alabama, and the railroad companies in most states, for example, were not backward in stating their position on such proposed measures as banking and currency, tariff, anti-trust, and child-labor legislation. As William E. Dodd wrote in 1920, ". . . the South had got just enough of the new industrialism and the profits of big business to disturb the thinking of her leaders." In that region, he continued, "although men were ardent Democrats, economic interests took precedence over any theories of democracy that formerly underlay their party attitude, at least that was true of their more experienced statesmen."

Nevertheless, the retreat of southern sectionalism has generally coincided with the appearance of Democratic administrations in Washington. Wilson was a strong President who did much to interest Southerners in national affairs and to pull southern politicians into the orbit of national politics. During the Wilson years local and state politicians in the South suddenly found themselves under strong pressure to endorse the President and his reforms. The Wilson administration also elicited growing recognition among Southerners of the fact that many problems were incapable of solution by city and state action, and must be dealt with by the national government.

Perhaps no one symbolizes the reciprocal nature of the relationship between Wilsonian politics and southern progressivism better than Josephus Daniels, the North Carolina editor who served as Secretary of the Navy throughout the Wilson years. As editor of the Raleigh *News and Observer*—the "Nuisance and Disturber" some people called it—Daniels had become a devoted supporter of Bryan and free silver in the mid-nineties. Probably no Southerner surpassed him as an exponent of Bryanism in the late nineties and early years of the twentieth century. An "apostle of righteous discontent" and an ardent and resourceful critic of big business, he carried on a tireless campaign against the Southern Railway Company and the American Tobacco Company. He condemned the practice of granting free passes, and the powerful railroad lobbies, while urging the establishment of a stronger railroad commission, lower railroad rates, strong anti-trust legislation, a more equitable tax system, and various other reforms, including state-wide prohibition.

Daniels was fixed in his loyalty to the Democratic party, yet he was a surpassing example of a southern progressive. This was reflected not only in his anti-corporation attitudes and economic radicalism, but also in his virulent Negrophobia. So lurid and sensational were his journalistic assaults on the fusionist government of North Carolina in the late nineties that his enemies derisively labeled him "the State Saviour." His efforts on behalf of Negro disfranchisement were cut from the same cloth, and from time to time in the years that followed the Tar Heel editor revealed the narrowness of his views in outbreaks like the Bassett affair at Trinity College. Nevertheless, there was a basic thread of consistency in Daniels' journalism and politics (the two were virtually indistinguishable). His son, looking back much later with affection and nostalgia at the confident years of the Wilson administration, remembered how as a small boy he had come to know his father's "faith as a democrat, spelled with a big and a little 'd.' He took it from Thomas Jefferson almost with the feeling that Jefferson had personally handed it to him." Daniels was "scornful of any supposed elite. He kept an almost mystic faith in the people themselves." His liberalism was no passing phenomenon. It remained with him—and it became more comprehensive as time passed. If Southerners like Josephus Daniels helped give a progressive character to the Wilson movement, the Wilson administration in turn swept many of them on to a broader kind of liberalism.

Daniels proved to be an able cabinet member. He attempted to purify and democratize the Navy as well as to make it more effective, and as Secretary he revealed his old fears of monopolies in his determined battles against the armor-plate manufacturers and the oil interests. In the 1920's Daniels, like Bryan, sometimes seemed to be an anachronistic figure out of a forgotten past. But he kept the lamp of his progressivism burning brightly. He fought the utility interests in North Carolina, supported government operation of Muscle Shoals, opposed the Ku Klux Klan, and defied many Democrats to back Alfred E. Smith's campaign in 1928. He was one of the early enthusiasts for the cause of Franklin D. Roosevelt, who owed a great debt to Daniels for having given him an appreciation of the agrarian liberalism the North Carolinian had long embodied. As E. David Cronon has pointed out, Daniels was a direct link between the simple Bryan agrarianism of the 1890's, the broader Wilson idealism of the progressive era, and the still more complex New Deal of Franklin D. Roosevelt.

The decline of the progressive movement during World War I, the foundering of Woodrow Wilson's peace plans on the shoals of partisanship and normalcy, and the overwhelming repudiation of the Democratic party in 1920, were reflected in the politics of the region from the Potomac to the Rio Grande. For one thing, the powerful current forcing southern politicians into places of power and responsibility in a national administration, with the attendant pressures on state and local leaders in the South, was gone. Liberals throughout the South felt the loss of Wilson's leadership. This is not to say that southern influence in the Democratic party declined. In fact, just the opposite occurred; with the decline of Democratic strength in other parts of the country Southerners could more nearly dominate the shaping of party policy than had been possible during the Wilson period. At the same time, a certain blandness began to assert itself in the region's politics, and the strong dual factionalism and durable cleavages of the prewar period threatened to disintegrate.

Yet the old factionalism did not entirely disappear, nor did progressivism completely die out. Toward the end of the twenties, the latent class conflict in Louisiana provided the setting for Huey P. Long, whose regime in turn established the basis for a durable and well-disciplined bifactional system. In the case of Louisiana it is worth noting that the agrarian revolt was more abortive and progressivism was less successful than in most southern states; the conservative political hierarchy, representing an efficient New Orleans machine, powerful commercial interests, and the plantation element, managed to rule the state for decades. The social reforms Long forced through were certainly overdue, and the impact of his leadership was extraordinarily great. As T. Harry Williams has written, "By

advancing issues that mattered to the masses and by repeal-
ing the poll tax, he stirred voter interest to a height un-
matched in any other Southern state, and he left Louisiana with an enduring bifactionalism that has many of the
attributes of a two-party system." "Perhaps the lesson of
Long," remarks Professor Williams, "is that if in a democracy needed changes are denied too long by an interested
minority, the changes, when they come, will come with a
measure of repression and revenge."

No other southern state experienced such a political upheaval. But throughout the South in the twenties some of
the old reformism was evident. It found a partial outlet
in the effort to enforce prohibition, an issue that had a
long history in southern politics. In a peculiarly satisfying
way, the growing agitation over the liquor question during the progressive era absorbed the yearnings for reform
and fulfillment of a people whose God had become Progress but whose ideas remained fundamentally conservative. No other proposal expressed the ambivalent desires
of the South so well, nor did any other so effectively combine the varied reform elements that were struggling to
express themselves.

In a broader way southern progressivism had been transformed by the 1920's from the more militant anti-corporation and political reform movement of the prewar period
to what George B. Tindall has aptly called "business progressivism." Even in earlier years the force of southern
progressivism was blunted by the widespread faith in industrial progress. "But now," Professor Tindall has written, "the term Progress appeared in a subtly different con-
text. It was more closely associated with the urban middle
class, with chambers of commerce and Rotary Clubs. It
carried the meaning of efficiency and development rather
than reform." It reflected the pervasive faith in the region's
economic progress and made the government a sort of

agent of industrial prosperity. This development was not unnatural. For if the 1880's represent the first real stirring of industrialism in the modern South, the 1920's stand out as a decade that vastly accelerated earlier industrial trends. Nor should we forget that "business progressivism" was nourished by Wilsonian liberalism: the New Freedom contained a pronounced entrepreneurial strain and many of the business progressives of the twenties had been ardent Wilsonians.

In terms of efficiency and the public service concept of government there was a surprisingly vigorous reform movement in the South during the 1920's. A series of constructive governors, including Cameron Morrison of North Carolina, Bibb Graves of Alabama, and Austin Peay of Tennessee, achieved notable success in expanding public services and modernizing the machinery of state government. The development of highway programs and improved systems of education was spectacular in several southern states. Most of the southern states made phenomenal increases in expenditures for state services, introduced tax reforms and found new sources of revenue, created new administrative departments, developed their public health programs, and made significant progress in establishing welfare programs—this despite much talk about economy in government and laissez faire. Thus it is far from accurate to picture southern politics in the twenties entirely in the somber colors of the Ku Klux Klan, prohibition, and Bible Belt fundamentalism, important as were those influences.

But while Southerners were expanding and rationalizing their state governments and endeavoring to transform the face of the land through economic changes, they held on grimly to old-time social and religious mores. As Donald Davidson put it some years later, "The United Daughters of the Confederacy and the Kiwanis Club flourished side by side. Mule-wagon and automobile, fundamentalism and liberalism, education and illiteracy, aristocratic pride and backwoods independence disproved the axiom that two bodies cannot occupy the same space. Cities that preserved the finest flavor of the old regime had to be approached over brand-new roads where bill-boards, tourist camps, filling stations, and factories broke out in a modernistic rash among the water oaks and Spanish moss." The fact is that the "business progressivism" of the more constructive political leaders ruffled the feathers of the region's social conservatives hardly at all. But the changes occurring in the character of the Democratic party on the national level certainly did. Although there were some economic differences between the South and West on the one hand, and the East on the other, the bitter conflict between urban and rural Democrats, roughly symbolized by the northeastern and southern leadership of the party, was not so much an economic as it was a social and cultural clash. Many Southerners rebelled against the incipient orientation of the Democratic party toward the urban, Catholic, and "wet" East.

If, as William E. Leuchtenburg contends, the 1920's were a time when the country as a whole first began to come to grips with the modern trends of industrialization, urbanization, and cultural pluralism, how much more difficult was this process of adjustment for the South, with an economy that was still largely agricultural, with an essentially rural and small-town culture, with a white population predominantly Protestant in religion and Anglo-Saxon in ethnic background. At any rate, the protracted struggle in the national convention of 1924 was only a prelude to the desertion of a Tammanyite presidential candidate four years later.

Meanwhile, southern Republicanism made some gains prior to the election of 1928. For the most part, however,

Southerners who might have turned to the Republican party during the twenties were satisfied with the business-oriented and forward-looking governments in states like Tennessee, Virginia, North Carolina, and Alabama, and with the passing of Bryan and Wilson they had less reason to be alarmed because of upsetting economic policies or liberal ideas emanating from the party's national leaders. Nevertheless, southern Republicanism had shown some modest increases, particularly in the election of 1920. In that contest Republican percentages went up in every southern state: the G. O. P. carried Tennessee (including the governorship) and Oklahoma, and it won ten congressional districts in those two states. Also, there were doubtless many Democrats in the same boat with the Arkansas lawyer who wrote, soon after the election of 1920, "I am one of the numerous Southern Democrats who voted for Cox and rejoiced in the election of Harding." Although the Republicans failed to make additional gains in 1924, possibly because of depressed agricultural conditions, it was becoming easier to think of Republican affiliations in a region so strongly committed to the gospel of business expansion and economic diversification. Republican leaders were aware of this and during the late twenties there was renewed talk of a strong Republican party in the South, encouraged no doubt by the threatened disruption of the southern Democracy. The efforts to make Republicanism more respectable in the South by transforming it into a "lily-white" party, a movement that had been under way for a generation or more, received new impetus.

While the issues were different and the social divisions confused, the fierceness of the intraparty battles in 1928 was reminiscent of the bitter struggles of the 1890's. But this time the dissenters made no attempt at third-party politics; instead they sought to capture control of the Democratic party machinery on the state and local levels and to swing their states to the Republicans in the presidential contest. The devices used in these efforts varied and sometimes were not very logical. Yet they succeeded in capturing Texas, Tennessee, North Carolina, Virginia, and Florida, as well as every border state, for the Republican presidential ticket. The Republicans almost carried Alabama. Significantly, Herbert Hoover's victories in the South did not occur in the areas of strongest rural, prohibition, and Protestant sentiment, but in those states with relatively few Negroes, traditional Republican strength, and economic interests that pulled them toward national integration. The old centers of southern sectionalism, the black belts, remained true to their Democratic faith.

Thus the period that began soon after the abortive Populist efforts to break the Solid South drew to a close a generation later with a Republican candidate for President carrying five southern states. It was a period in which, except for the border states, every southern state was so wedded to the Democratic party that any break in its solidarity on the state and national levels was almost unthinkable. It was a period, moreover, in which the southern handling of the race issue encountered little interference from Congress or President, found few challenges in the federal courts, and received the general approbation of public opinion in the country at large. Even a liberal Democratic administration on the national scene served, ironically, to increase the region's attachment to the Democratic party.

On the other hand, important developments during these years contributed to the promise of a more democratic politics for the South. A strong bifactionalism emerged along liberal-conservative lines. A significant farm movement influenced the making of public policies, and an important middle-of-the-road progressivism appeared with an urban leadership and philosophy. The result was the enactment during the progressive era and in the 1920's of many social reforms and the introduction of numerous public services. Meanwhile, the South was being further differentiated in its economy and society by industrialization and urbanization, the rapid growth of Texas and Oklahoma and their divergence in many ways from the rest of the South, and the economic diversification of the upper South. At the same time, the South's social conservatism and its long one-party habit made its sectionalism a strong force in the national struggles of the twenties.

Yet these were truly the mid-passage years for the Solid South. Southerners might call the results of the 1928 election an aberration, and in a sense they were, but it is clear that the real explanation lies in fundamental pressures long accumulating in the nation at large and in the South. The most obvious thing was the changing character of the Democratic party on the national scene. Equally portentous for the Solid South were the changes in the pattern of economic and social life in many parts of the South itself.

frightened the conservatives, shocked the section out of its normal complacency toward national politics, promoted the growth of organized labor, and encouraged the spread of liberal ideas throughout the South. The destructiveness of the depression and the encouragement of the New Deal brought the first real stirring of the southern "proletariat" —of submerged elements like the sharecropper, the textile worker, and the Negro domestic servant. It introduced codes and standards that did much to undermine the old faith in freedom of contract and state rights. Those who opposed what they considered to be federal encroachments on state rights learned that they must assume responsibilities on the state level if they were to head off centralization.

Most Southerners, however, seemed willing enough to accept federal aid. Indeed, their interest in this side of American federalism long antedated the New Deal, and it was expressed by conservatives and liberals alike. As a southern political scientist wrote in 1931, "The seeking of Federal aid for southern highways, flood control, barge service, or cotton marketing, is only one aspect of the southern policy of looking northward for public and private funds for economic, scientific, and cultural development." During the depression state rights seemed less essential than federal assistance, and especially so since many of the New Deal programs benefited the South more than other parts of the country and since the benefits the section received far surpassed the contributions Southerners made to federal revenue collections. There was more than a little truth in William Faulkner's later assertion: "We— Mississippi—sold our state's rights back to the federal government when we accepted the first cotton price-support subsidy twenty years ago. Our economy is not agricultural any longer. Our economy is the federal government.

We no longer farm in Mississippi cotton fields. We farm now in Washington corridors and Congressional committee rooms."

The point needs to be made that some of this federal money was being spent to ease the plight of the most oppressed elements in southern society. While this was true all over the United States, in no other section was federal intervention as momentous in its implications as in the South. For in that area tenant farmers, mill workers, Negroes, and mountaineers had suffered so long and severely from their marginal position in the southern economy, not to mention their cultural and political disadvantages, as to convince most of them that there was no relief to be had short of providential intervention. In a sense the New Deal was the realization of all the old dreams that looked to the national government for assistance in helping a depressed section and the depressed groups in its population to get on their feet—the economic and educational needs of the freedmen during Reconstruction, the aims of the Blair education bill in the 1880's, the governmental policies of the agrarian radicals in the 1890's, and the continued pleas of farmers for aid in the 1920's.

To Southerners, perhaps even more than to other Americans, the New Deal was symbolized by the leadership of Franklin D. Roosevelt. The President's interest in people as individuals, his understanding of the existence of the past in the present, and the way in which he identified himself with the southern region struck a responsive chord among Southerners, who had always tended to personalize relationships and to approach matters of government on a person-to-person basis. While maintaining a high degree of personal popularity among southern congressmen, Roosevelt also captured the minds and hearts of the southern masses. "Roosevelt," blurted an exasperated North Carolina mill worker to an anti-New Deal reporter, "is the only man we ever had in the White House who would understand that my boss is a sonofabitch."

During the New Deal years Roosevelt's leadership tended to broaden and nationalize the outlook of southern congressmen, much as had Wilson's administration. At the same time, Roosevelt demonstrated his independence of the Democratic South by his powerful appeal to the masses of voters in other regions, and he even forced the South to acknowledge its loss of indispensability to the party by accepting the repeal of the historic two-thirds rule in the national convention of 1936.

But the relationship between the New Deal and southern Democrats worked both ways, for the President found that he still had to depend upon the co-operation of southern party leaders, who once more monopolized the important committee chairmanships, in the enactment of his program. Some southern leaders, in fact, played important and constructive roles in the passage of New Deal legislation, including such men as Joseph T. Robinson, Hugo L. Black, Alben W. Barkley, William B. Bankhead, and Sam Rayburn. The liberalism of these men—and that of younger congressmen like Maury Maverick and Lyndon B. Johnson—was fortified and made more effective by the Roosevelt administration. But it is easy to lose sight of the fact that the leadership of many southern congressmen during the New Deal years also reflected the liberal tendencies of their constituents.

The Roosevelt administration also had its influence on the Democratic factionalism of the southern states, since it forced New Deal issues into state and local political contests. Almost all of the southern states felt the impact of New Deal policies in their state administrations, for reforms and new public services at this level were stimulated and often directly promoted by national legislation. Long-needed legislation was enacted, and some southern states, such as Georgia under E. D. Rivers, inaugurated "Little New Deal" programs. Other leaders, such as Eugene Talmadge and W. Lee O'Daniel, sounded the old notes of agrarian radicalism in the thirties but frequently turned out to be conservative in everything except campaign techniques.

The abrogation of the two-thirds rule and, especially, Roosevelt's attack on the Supreme Court unsettled many of the southern congressmen and gave them an excuse to oppose the administration. The threat of an anti-lynching bill and the last major reform surge of the New Deal in 1937-1938 precipitated increasing opposition from southern congressional leaders like Walter F. George and Carter Glass. Many of these men spoke for southern business interests, and their bitter opposition to such New Deal measures as the wages and hours bill in 1937-1938 reflected the South's fear that it would lose certain regional advantages in its efforts to industrialize. Roosevelt's one real effort to take an active hand in eliminating some of the more obdurate southern conservatives came in the congressional elections of 1938; it failed and the administration's drive for domestic reform was soon engulfed in the larger concern with World War II.

The mounting opposition to the New Deal by conservative Southerners in the late thirties and early forties was, to some extent, an indication of the revival of business hopes in the region and an assertion by its politicians of their old-time independence in national affairs. But it was more than that. The pragmatic southern congressmen had not been entirely unsuccessful in tempering the more radical features of New Deal legislation, and the Roosevelt administration had been forced, insofar as its hopes for a far-reaching revolution in the South were concerned, to come to terms with the conservatives who controlled the section's politics, economy, and social life.

Yet if the New Deal did not dislodge those who dominated the power structure in the South, it threatened them as they had never been threatened before—and in this respect it was unlike the New Freedom of Woodrow Wilson, which the conservative South made peace with, or even the Populist revolt, which for all of its threatening aspects was quickly overcome and used to prevent insurrection in the future. The New Deal was different. Try as politicians might—by joining it for a time, by endeavoring to water down its program, by resorting to subterfuge, ingenious arguments, and clever appeals to old-time shibboleths—the threat remained, and it promised to grow larger in the future. Not only did it seem more and more unlikely that the South could ever dominate the Democratic party again, but it was also increasingly apparent that the national policies adopted during the thirties would ultimately strengthen organized labor, farmers, Negroes, and middle-class people sufficiently to force concessions from those who had long had the upper hand in the region. This was the real measure of the New Deal's challenge to southern conservatives.

The war, which was strongly supported by Southerners, moderated southern discontent with certain aspects of the administration's program. Party loyalty and economic considerations involving foreign trade, as well as such factors as military tradition, ethnic composition, and psychological make-up, stimulated southern internationalism. The war boom, moreover, served as a mighty force in rejuvenating the southern economy and providing it with a more substantial foundation than the old cotton economy. Nevertheless, while supporting the war, large numbers of southern congressmen opposed many of the President's proposals, reassured no doubt by his failure in the 1938 "purge" effort and encouraged by his difficulties since that time. The defeat of many northern Democratic congressmen in 1942 and 1946 further strengthened the influence of the southern conservatives in the party, and Roosevelt's death, which temporarily cast southern liberals adrift, added to this supremacy. In the early forties, moreover, a group of southern anti-New Deal governors, led by Eugene Talmadge and Sam Houston Jones, launched violent attacks on various parts of Roosevelt's program.

Southern liberals did not disappear entirely from Congress and state politics during the forties and early fifties, however, and there were rather distinctive liberal-conservative cleavages in the region that revolved around New Deal-Fair Deal issues. Although a definite trend toward conservatism in state politics in the South was apparent after 1940, in virtually every southern commonwealth a liberal faction inspired by and oriented toward the national administration struggled against the control of the conservatives. Young Ellis G. Arnall of Georgia won a notable record for progressivism during the war years, and in the postwar period Kerr Scott of North Carolina and Sidney S. McMath of Arkansas provide examples of southern governors in the New Deal tradition who achieved considerable success. Proven liberals like Claude Pepper, Lister Hill, Brooks Hays, and Estes Kefauver continued in Congress. Private groups like the Southern Conference for Human Welfare, organized in the late thirties, expressed the liberal Southerner's desire for a broad program of social action to elevate the region. During the first three or four years following the war a great many Southerners still thought of themselves as New Deal Democrats, and there was a strong idealization of FDR among the masses of southern people. But the manner in which the coalition between southern Democratic congressmen and

Republican representatives operated seemed to belie the region's devotion to New Deal liberalism. President Truman's forthright advocacy of a civil rights program caused many to draw back and allowed those who wanted to repudiate the national administration, for whatever reason, to seize the initiative.

Furthermore, as the forties ended and the fifties began the contours of southern politics were undergoing a significant alteration. To some extent this development in the politics of the South mirrored the growing conservatism and spirit of moderation that characterized the nation as a whole. But there was more to it than that. Perhaps the most important manifestation of what was happening in the South was the declining importance, at least in state politics, of the strong bifactionalism and of the old economic and geographic divisions. In many ways this was reminiscent of what happened in the 1920's.

In the first place, there is good reason to believe that a new and stronger group politics in the region had not yet been assimilated by the old bifactional system. But at the same time southern political leaders seemed to be trying to adjust to the new politics. In several states they broadened their appeal to the electorate by emphasizing the public service concept of government. Although many state legislators, especially those from rural areas, continued to reflect the ancient faith in a parsimonious and limited government, state leaders who adamantly opposed social change and advocated a negative government of retrenchment, state rights, and extreme individualism tended to pass from the scene. The death of Talmadge in Georgia and the overthrow of Edward H. Crump in Tennessee also disrupted the dual factionalism which had long characterized the politics of those two states. In the second place, the social conservatism of the South reasserted itself vigorously in the controversies over civil rights and school integration (like prohibition and religious fundamentalism in the twenties). The short-run consequences of both developments appeared to be a politics of blandness and considerable white unity on the state level. But even in this situation the position of the party leaders and of white Southerners generally was not unrelated to important socio-economic changes taking place in the region.

The Dixiecrat movement in 1948 and subsequent Republican successes in the South were the culmination of two streams of protest which had been building up against the Roosevelt and Truman administrations since the thirties. Many Southerners responded to the States Rights Democrats because of their hostility toward New Deal economic policies. But despite its tender regard for business interests and its effort to refurbish the arguments for state rights and constitutional government, the Dixiecrat movement gathered most of its strength from the racism and traditional sectionalism that had always frustrated political realignment and perpetuated the Solid South.

The States Righters enjoyed their greatest success in those black belt areas which V. O. Key describes as the hard core of the Solid South, the areas that had stood by the Democrats in 1928. Long disturbed by the New Deal's "coddling" of the Negro, and troubled by the implications of American war aims as well as by such wartime innovations as the federal commission on employment practices, many Southerners had their worst fears realized in Truman's civil rights recommendations. The southern leaders apparently hoped that Truman would be more responsive to the "southern bloc" in Congress. They assumed that he would be defeated in 1948 and, having foreseen that northern liberals would raise the civil rights issue in the national convention, they seized upon the election as a favorable time to frighten the party leadership into a more co-operative attitude. In the process they doubtless hoped to smash their liberal opponents in the South by forcing them to endorse the unpopular side of the race issue and align themselves with the national party on that question.

Yet perhaps the most significant thing about the Dixiecrat revolt was its failure—a failure that came in spite of fervent appeals to the South's most cherished traditions. Even in Alabama, Louisiana, Mississippi, and South Carolina, the states which they carried, the States Righters appropriated the official Democratic label on the ballot. Despite their contention that the Democratic party in such states was a political organization independent of the national party, they were cast in the unfamiliar role of insurgents, of bolters. They failed to heed the lessons of 1928. The most substantial political leaders in the region shied away from the Dixiecrat radicals and were careful to keep lines of communication open with the national party leadership. Following the election the question of party loyalty became an issue in some southern states along the general lines of the old liberal-conservative cleavage. The fact that white-supremacy politicians like Herman Talmadge and Olin D. Johnston would have no part of the third-party movement indicated the anachronistic character of the old sectionalism. No politician interested in national politics could afford to campaign on such a sectional basis. Sectional politics could not control national politics, but rather must be adjusted to it. Most issues had become national issues, and the major social and economic divisions extended throughout the country, causing Southerners and Northerners to be arrayed against Southerners and Northerners. As H. C. Nixon said some years ago, "In our political arithmetic national denominators are gaining in importance in comparison with regional denominators."

If the Dixiecrat movement of 1948 gave expression to pressures serving to retard political change in the South, the national elections of the 1950's reflected long-accumulating forces pushing toward political realignment in the region. What happened in 1952 and 1956 was not unrelated to the schism of 1948, for there was a noticeable "Dixiecrat to Ike" trend in the states that had been carried by J. Strom Thurmond. (On a smaller scale there was also a States Rights to Republican shift in 1960.) In some cases the Dixiecrat ticket became a halfway house along the road to Republicanism. But the basic explanation of the Republican victories in the South lies in the long dissatisfaction, primarily for economic reasons, on the part of many southern Democrats with New Deal policies. This southern distaste for New Deal liberalism had already begun to reveal itself in such sporadic movements as the "Constitutional Democrats of Texas" in 1936, the "Jeffersonian Democratic Party" of South Carolina in 1940, and the "Texas Regulars" in 1944. By 1952 this Democratic discontent had grown strong enough to burst its old bounds in vigorous fashion, and in doing so revealed some of the deep-seated economic and social forces on which it rested.

The most significant of the new factors in southern politics are associated with the economic revolution that is industrializing and urbanizing the South, diversifying its economy, and effecting a large migration into and out of its borders. The South's relative position among the major regions has improved in almost every category of wealth since 1930. Factories and assembly plants have sprung up from Richmond to San Antonio; agriculture has been increasingly mechanized and diversified; sharecroppers and agricultural workers in large numbers have left the farms for the cities of the North and South, while a growing stream of technicians, managers, and businessmen has flowed into the region. By mid-century less than one out of every five southern workers was employed in agriculture, and by that time cotton had declined in importance to such an extent that it furnished no more than one-fourth of the South's farm income. Will Rogers observed many years earlier that "the Yankees are swarming into the South like locusts," and that "the rascals bring their Republican politics with 'em." In more recent years the saying is that "Cotton is going West, cattle are coming East, Negroes are going North, and Yankees are coming South." A broad new middle class, as well as a liberal sprinkling of *nouveau riche,* has emerged in the cities, which are now growing at a faster rate than those of the Northeast. Between 1930 and 1950, for example, the growth of cities of 50,000 or more people in the South proceeded at a rate three times the national average. As late as 1920 the South was only about one-fourth urban. Today more than half of all Southerners live in urban communities.

Despite their assiduous efforts to industrialize their section, Southerners frequently argue that economic innovations need not change their social and political institutions. Yet the economic revolution in the South is surely introducing new ideas and new habits diluting the homogeneity of the region, breaking the cake of social custom, and creating a society that will become more impervious to the debilitating effects of white-supremacy politics. Greater general prosperity and new modes of urban life will almost certainly have an impact upon a political system in which great numbers of people previously have been too poor and apathetic to play any part. The city provides better schools and better jobs and it facilitates the group approach to politics. In the urban South workers have a better opportunity to join labor unions and Negroes begin to vote; people join organizations and some of them become civic minded and politically conscious for the first time. In effect the city increasingly is providing more and more of the South's traditionally underrepresented elements with a new and more democratic political setting. It is already apparent, as Alexander Heard has noted, that these developments are creating divisive elements in southern politics and sharpening social and economic issues in such a way as to cut into the traditional domination of the black belts. Negroes, farmers, and urban workers in a state like Texas are not inclined to vote for the same policies as the "respectable" and wealthy people.

The clearest manifestation of all this can be found in the national elections of the 1950's. When viewed against the background of a changing South, the Republican victories of 1952 and 1956 (and 1960 as well) in the region become far more than Eisenhower victories, though many Southerners rationalized their Republican votes on the ground that General Eisenhower was above party, or by asserting that there were no real differences between the two parties—only between their candidates. Republican successes represent what Professor Key calls "the political fulfillment of demographic and economic trends" south of the Potomac. Although the number of "Presidential Republicans" in the South increased in the 1940's, the election of 1952 was the event that set off the explosive forces long building up there.

The most significant thing about 1952 is not that it inaugurated a real two-party system in the South, which is clearly not the case, but that an analysis of the election returns shows that Southerners, especially in the cities, divided their votes much as did other Americans and for essentially the same reasons. In city after city in the southern states Eisenhower carried the upper-income precincts by handsome majorities (and a great many of the middle-income precincts by less generous majorities), while Adlai E. Stevenson carried the lower-income districts by equally substantial margins. In 1956 the Republicans carried no less than sixty of the approximately one hundred urban counties in the eleven ex-Confederate states. In two out of every three southern counties containing a city of at least 25,000 people, the Republicans actually increased their percentage of the vote over 1952. While their percentages declined somewhat in 1960, the same pattern emerges from an analysis of the returns from that election. In the sixty-eight metropolitan counties and independent cities (those with an urban population of 50,000 or more) in the former Confederate states, Richard M. Nixon received 49.3 per cent of the total vote as compared with 47.8 per cent for John F. Kennedy. Nixon probably benefited to some extent from Kennedy's Catholic religion, particularly in Tennessee and Oklahoma, and it should be noted that he ran better than Eisenhower in the black belts of six southern states. But fundamentally the southern voters were motivated by social and economic considerations—and party habit and loyalty, of course.

A recent study of political behavior in a representative "white" precinct in a southern city suggests that President Eisenhower's personality appeal did not operate in a random fashion among Dixie Democrats. Such factors as socioeconomic status, migration patterns, and issue orientation revealed differences between what the authors call "Eisencrats" and "Stevencrats." Loyalty to the Democratic party remains a major consideration in southern politics, but changes in class identification are clearly laying the groundwork for shifts in party affiliation. Some evidence of this can be found in another significant aspect of the Republican victories in the South: the way in which the recurrent cleavages within the Democratic party in the southern states spilled over into the national contests between the major parties. In Louisiana, for example, the Long forces supported Stevenson while the anti-Long voters crossed party lines in large numbers to cast their ballots for Eisenhower. In Texas the Republican vote in 1952 and 1956 was similar to the Shivers vote in 1954 and the anti-regular vote in 1958. Even in Florida, where a multifactional system has long prevailed, the traditional liberal-conservative division in Democratic primaries is being translated into a Democratic-Republican division in national elections.

The return of Negroes to the polls during recent years is another development that is full of significance for southern politics. The large increase of Negro voters in the South following the famous *Smith v. Allwright* decision of 1944, which opened the white primaries to members of that race, represents a revolution in southern voting habits. More than 163,000 Negroes had registered in Georgia by the end of 1956, as compared with only 10,000 in 1944. The Southern Regional Council estimated that Negro registration in the former Confederate states had risen to 1,238,000 by the last part of 1956. Despite these impressive gains, only about 26 per cent of the southern Negroes of voting age are registered today, as compared with 60 per cent of the eligible whites. Furthermore, Negro registration varies widely in the South (and within the individual southern states)—from 6 per cent of the adult Negro population in Mississippi to 48 per cent in Tennessee.

Since the mid-fifties the pace of Negro registration has perceptibly slowed, possibly because most of the middle-class and better-educated Negroes had registered by that time. Certainly poverty and illiteracy, apathy and indifference, and lack of leadership are stout barriers to the political involvement of the Negro masses, as they are to the political activation of many whites. But many Negroes in the Deep South who are qualified to register have been prevented from doing so by the subterfuges of white leaders and the social and economic pressures of white communities.

Yet the situation is not without promise. Both the Eisenhower and the Kennedy administrations have taken

legal action under the civil rights legislation of 1957 and
1960 to force registrars and other responsible officials to
permit qualified Negroes to vote. The Kennedy administration seems to be especially sanguine about the possibility of bringing a new political complexion to the South
through Negro voting, and it is now supporting a region-
wide registration campaign which is being co-ordinated by
the Southern Regional Council. The anti-poll tax amend-
ment may remove one of the hoariest obstacles to Negro
voting in some southern states. Meanwhile, the appearance of numerous Negro voting leagues and the new note
of militancy among Negro leaders suggest that the ballot
has become one of the most cherished symbols in the
Negro's long quest for equality. Finally, in this whole matter the Southerner's Americanism will inevitably frustrate
his Southernism, for it is increasingly obvious that the
white Southerner can make no legitimate defense of political discrimination based on race, whatever his darker
visions of racial amalgamation may be, and fewer and
fewer make any such attempt.

Although the Negro vote in the South has not become
the balance of power the demagogue spoke of in his old-
time warning, it has become too important to ignore. A
student of Louisiana politics has pointed out, for instance,
that it is "statistically provable that the Negro vote was a
crucial element in Adlai Stevenson's narrow victory in
Louisiana in 1952; in Earl Long's first primary triumph
in the 1956 Democratic gubernatorial primary; and in
Eisenhower's precedent-shattering conquest of Louisiana's
electoral vote in 1956."

One of the most drastic shifts in the presidential election returns of 1956, as compared with 1952, was the
manner in which Negro voters left the Democratic party
to support the Republicans. This shift was nowhere more
pronounced than in the South, where civil rights and the

slogan, "A vote for the Democrats is a vote for Eastland," proved effective in overcoming the attraction of economic considerations offered by the Democrats. In other words, Negro Southerners, like white Southerners, were caught between social (or racial) and economic pressures in deciding how to vote. In twenty-three southern cities Negroes increased their vote for Eisenhower and Nixon by 36.8 per cent over 1952. In 1952 Stevenson carried the Negro precincts in Atlanta by more than two to one, but four years later he received less than 15 per cent of the votes in those precincts.

In 1960 Negro voters returned to the Democratic standard in large numbers; indeed, they may have been an indispensable element in Kennedy's narrow victory. They were certainly the difference in a number of closely-contested states, including Illinois, Michigan, and South Carolina. In the last state an estimated 40,000 Negroes voted for Kennedy, who carried the state by a margin of 10,000 votes!

Urban politics in particular reflect the Negro's new political role. Negroes have been elected members of city councils and school boards,* Southerners of darker skin have suddenly begun to acquire an unaccustomed leverage in obtaining a fairer share of municipal services, and local politicians increasingly are taking Negro voters into account. As one Florida Negro put it at a voting league rally: "There's one thing the Negro has that the white man wants but can't get unless you give it to him. That's your vote." In a story on the progress that Richmond, Virginia, has made in desegregation and non-discrimination, a Washington *Post* reporter recently wrote: "The Negro vote, once the kiss of death, now is an asset; no

---

*In 1962 Leroy A. Johnson, an Atlanta Negro, was elected as a Democrat to the state senate of Georgia. He is the first Negro to win such a seat in over half a century.

candidate for City Council can afford to offend it and expect to win."

Looking ahead to the time when Negroes will be more adequately represented in the voting population of the South, Louis E. Lomax in *The Negro Revolt* pictures two southern Senators meeting outside the Senate chamber at the end of a busy day. They talk. Mississippi Senator: "By God, niggers are voting in my state." Alabama Senator: "Hell, they are voting in mine too; and furthermore, they ain't niggers, they are colored citizens." The mere fact that southern Negroes are voting in appreciable numbers is full of meaning, but it may be equally significant to note that they tend to join the liberal factions of the Democratic party. It was almost as if another of the old Populist dreams was coming true. Fifty years ago W. E. B. Du Bois declared that "The Negro voter . . . has in his hand the tremendous power of emancipating the Democratic Party from its enslavement to the reactionary South." Whether Du Bois was remarkably prescient or whether he was merely tempting the irony of fate, in today's setting his analysis contains a good deal of truth.

Lest it be assumed that these observations are meant to suggest the imminent appearance of a dynamic two-party system in the South, it would be well at this point to consider the obstacles that stand in the path of a more realistic southern politics. In this connection, we should not underestimate the importance of the ancient symbols. The South's history shows how powerful tradition can be in the realm of political ideas and behavior. Those automobile stickers in 1952 proclaiming "I'm a Democrat but I like Ike" had their own special meaning. There is still much truth in what Virginius Dabney wrote in 1942. "Many Southerners who currently profess allegiance to the Democratic party," observed Dabney, "would be far more congenially situated as Republicans if they could but forget Thad Stevens and Ben Wade, and put out of their minds the fact that to their grandfathers the Democratic party was only slightly less sacrosanct than the Army of Northern Virginia."

Racial tension since World War II and the "New Know Nothingism" in the South have helped to gloss over the economic and social divisions in many political contests and to impede the incipient transformation of southern politics. The manner in which some southern members of labor unions have behaved during race relations crises of recent years demonstrates that the region's social conservatism continues to obstruct its liberal economic and political tendencies. Many white Southerners find it difficult to resist the campaigns of racist rabble rousers. The Arkansas gubernatorial primary of 1958 provides an excellent example. In a campaign in which Little Rock and school integration overshadowed all other issues, Orval E. Faubus, who had faced a bleak political future less than a year before, was swept back into office by theatrically wrapping himself in the mantle of white supremacy. In Virginia the respectable Byrd machine, threatened on the left by liberal Democrats and on the right by a revived Republican party, suddenly discovered that school segregation was the magic road to white solidarity in the state.

As might be expected, Negrophobia as an ingredient in state politics is most widespread and blatant in the Deep South. Yet the politicians in these states no longer have any illusions about the possibility of unifying the South on the basis of anti-Negro appeals. And the very existence of the racial crisis, so often foretold by southern politicians, is an illustration of the way in which national and international pressures are working to bring provincial practices into line with American ideals. Furthermore, the identification in the southern mind of the national Democratic party with the Negro's drive for equal rights and the growing

Negro vote in the region's primaries may reverse the pattern of Reconstruction and persuade more and more white Southerners to affiliate with the Republican party.*

Another obstacle to a more democratic politics in the South stems from the disproportionate political power and the reactionary policies of many rural areas. Some observers have pointed out that the most pro-segregation agitation in the school controversy has been brought about by the inhabitants or spokesmen of regions of relative or absolute decline in population, unbalanced economy, and chronic problems of community or countryside. Ninety-eight of Georgia's 159 counties, for example, lost population in the 1940's, and 95 of them continued to decline during the next decade. Adverse economic and demographic forces have baffled and frustrated many rural people, exacerbating their fears of social change and their bitter hostility toward the city. Their declining economic and social status has made them more than ever the great conservators of the South's traditions, and they have lost much of the economic radicalism that once made them the cutting edge of southern reform. In this situation may be found part of the explanation for the upsurge of isolationism and opposition to internationalism as reflected in the position of many southern congressmen on foreign aid and other international questions.

It should be noted that this is not entirely a southern problem. The exaggerated influence of rural areas, perpetuated by out-of-date apportionment practices, is a problem almost everywhere. In fact, the most fundamental political problems in the South today are not vastly differ-

---

*This seems to be what happened in Alabama in 1962, when James D. Martin, the Republican candidate for the United States Senate, came within a few thousand votes of defeating Senator Lister Hill. Although Hill condemned President Kennedy's use of troops to enforce desegregation at the University of Mississippi, Martin campaigned against the Senator as the "Number One Kennedy Man" in the South.

ent from the fundamental political problems in other parts of the United States. It is true that few areas in the South have a competitive party system, but "one-partyism" is far from being a monopoly of the southern states. Perhaps no more than half of the states outside the South have a real two-party system; and in many of those that have, responsible government is consistently frustrated by the divided control guaranteed through staggered elections, the bicameral system, and the separation of powers. The absence of a responsible opposition party and the lack of interest and participation by most voters in state government seem to be characteristic of a majority of the states, North and South. The problem everywhere is how to quicken the interest of the voters in state politics, how to recruit able people to go into state and local government, and how to make the political process at these levels more responsive to the actual differences and divisions of the people and to the majority opinion. The persistent failure to secure responsible government on the state and local levels has been a major cause of political centralization in the United States.

In considering the chance of a two-party South, there is also a practical question to be kept in mind. Except for the presidency, why should conservatives in the South vote for the Republican opponents of men like Harry Flood Byrd and Richard B. Russell? Why, especially, when these and many less responsible southern congressmen, operating from powerful committee positions, have so often allied themselves with Republicans in Congress on questions that involve federal spending and domestic welfare programs? Who can deny that the real genius of the southern politician, both in Congress and elsewhere, is a genius of negative statecraft—of parliamentary skill and legislative mastery used to delay, to obstruct, to defeat, rather than to promote, to enact, to build—and that this more often than not is the very embodiment of conservative hopes? The extent and the effectiveness of the southern Democratic-Republican coalition may have been exaggerated, but it has scored some telling victories for the conservative cause—ranging from the destruction of the O.P.A. in 1946 to the frustration of several important domestic reforms sponsored by the Kennedy administration. In voting with Republicans in such a conservative vein southern congressmen are not altogether derelict in representing their constituents. To some extent they are reflecting a widespread feeling in the South that the odds in the fight for industrial development and economic prosperity have finally swung in their favor. Why even the odds? Or disturb a favorable situation? This attitude is certainly a factor in the growing Dixie revolt against the reciprocal trade program, which finds some southern politicians talking like latter-day William McKinleys.

As long as conservatives who call themselves Democrats can control the state governments in the South, there is no place for a separate conservative party led by Republicans. For the most part, Republican leaders, satisfied with Democratic control on the state level and primarily interested in convention politics and patronage from Washington, have not wanted to win elections at home. They are handicapped, moreover, by discriminatory election machinery, gerrymandering, undemocratic apportionment practices, nonpartisan municipal elections, and the like. Significant as were the Republican successes in the fifties, it is well to remember that few Republican congressmen and local officials were elected in the South during those years. Meanwhile the southern liberals, forced for so long into a procrustean bed with the dominant conservatives, have no alternative but to continue their support of the one-party system. Their polestar must remain the Democratic party at the national level.

In the final analysis, the fortunes of the Democratic party outside of the South will have much to do with southern politics. While the South has continued to be an important part of the Democratic party, the region has been unable since the 1920's to dominate the party's national conventions or to write its conservative philosophy into the national platforms and campaign documents. The "Al Smith Revolution" and Roosevelt's New Deal coalition made that impossible. A resurgent Democracy in the western and northern states will almost certainly impose its will on the party more vigorously than in the past, despite the Southerners' parliamentary adroitness. This would encourage southern liberals and make the Republican party more attractive in the eyes of many conservatives in the region. Despite the persistence of sectionalism, there is less and less need to be a crypto-Republican. According to a Mississippi congressman, writing in 1955 about southern politics during the past decade, "The one big change is the increasing respectability of the Republican party." Future Republican successes will also depend upon the priority assigned to the region by national party leaders and to the caliber of its leadership within the states. In the rim states of the South during recent years there has been a slow but definite increase in the number of state and local offices being contested by Republicans, as well as a modest increase in the percentage of votes polled by Republican candidates in congressional and state elections. In Texas, to cite a spectacular example, the G.O.P. in 1962 has entered candidates in eighteen of twenty-three congressional districts and in contests for over half of the seats in the state house of representatives. During the next few years Republican gains in the South probably will come primarily on the national level, with occasional state and congressional victories occurring first in such border states as North Carolina, Tennessee, Texas, and Florida, where the party is organized, has considerable strength, and benefits from economic and social conditions most favorable to political change.*

A wise Southerner has recently reminded us that the Solid South has always been "cracking from within." Until recently these cracks have not been very noticeable from the outside. But since 1948 the South has divided its electoral college votes in four straight elections; it can no longer be called a one-party region in national elections. There will surely be lasting effects from the shock produced by these divisive contests, no matter what the immediate future of southern Republicanism may be. Experience in other parts of the country suggests that the ending of the South's isolation from presidential campaigns will stimulate voting and citizen interest in state and local politics. Republican victories in the South were fundamentally the result of profound economic and social changes, which have been especially great since the 1930's. Under the impact of an economic revolution, a world war, and the New Deal, the last quarter of a century has witnessed the steady "erosion of sectionalism" in the southern states. Urbanization, industrialization, and the movement of people across the face of the country are undermining the old sectional attitudes and pointing toward a more complete political integration of all parts of the country. While retaining many of its accustomed habits and beliefs, the South has reflected the increasing homogenization of American society.

At the same time the South has become more and more

---

*In the elections of 1962 the Republicans in the South increased their strength in the national House of Representatives by winning four new seats, one each in Tennessee, North Carolina, Florida, and Texas. Henry Bellmon, the G.O.P. candidate for governor in Oklahoma, became the first Republican governor of that state. The Republican gubernatorial candidate in Texas received approximately 45 per cent of the votes cast in that state's election.

differentiated within itself. It is this development that really explains the growth of Republicanism in the region —and provides a more democratic basis for southern politics. As the editor of the *Texas Observer* pointed out a short time ago, "If a vital, functioning Republican party should emerge, then the dominant voice in the Texas Democratic party would become that of the classic Democratic coalition—East Texas farmers and city Negroes, Latin Americans, organized labor, the more general breed of 'brass-collar' Democrats and liberal intellectuals." In other words, the appearance of new class and group interests in a state like Texas may indicate a good chance to effect, on the foundations of the old liberal-conservative cleavages in the Democratic party, significant changes in southern politics. And as the urban populations come to exert greater weight in the political process through reapportionment and the political activation of the less affluent social elements, it is reasonable to expect southern politicians at all levels of government to broaden their programs and a more democratic politics to emerge.

If changing patterns of economic enterprise, social mobility, and population movement are causing southern society to become more diversified and differentiated, they are also bringing about modifications along geographical lines. This is most apparent in the upper part of the region, in the Southwest, and in Florida, although there is some evidence of the same phenomenon in the Deep South in intrastate sectionalism and the emergence of great urban complexes like Atlanta. What is happening in these states represents a progressive splintering of the once Solid South, with the historic cleavage between the upper and lower South being supplemented by new cracks in the wall of southern solidarity in the form of Florida's transformation into a land of sun-worshippers and retired people, and the increasing manifestation of western ideas and values in Texas and Oklahoma. These rim states have developed diversified economies, have smaller percentages of Negroes than the inner South, and have enough Republicanism to provide the basis for a real two-party system. This is particularly true in North Carolina, which has long had a large number of Republicans in its population and a Republican party that has contested congressional and state-wide offices for many years. The Negro voter is a factor of importance in each of these states, and the white people and their political leaders have increasingly accepted Negro participation in politics as right and even desirable. Although the machine in Virginia attempted to stay the hand of progress in race relations, its program of "massive resistance" collapsed, and it is apparent from recent primary elections in these states—and possibly in Arkansas as well—that the race issue is dead as a state-wide question. It was one of these states—Tennessee—that provided the first presidential bid by a Southerner in modern history on the basis of a genuine national appeal.

In pondering the political future of these southern states that give some evidence of breaking loose from their ancient moorings, it may be instructive to examine the experience of the border states: Kentucky, Maryland, West Virginia, and Missouri. For these middle states—and Oklahoma as well—whose economy and people were historically so southern and yet so northern may well have followed a political course that will be substantially duplicated by more and more southern states as they undergo social and economic changes. This is the opinion, at any rate, of John H. Fenton in his perceptive study of political trends in the border states. Following the Civil War, the Democrats captured control in all of these states. But in each of them the Republicans were strong enough to pose a constant threat and occasionally to defeat the Democrats when the latter's factionalism flared up in bitter controversies. In time a party realignment, reflecting economic and demographic trends as well as New Deal politics, brought most of the Negroes, many of the upland inhabitants, and the laboring classes in the industrial region into the Democratic party, while the business interests and the old Democratic Bourbon element, originally Whig, increasingly went over to the Republican party. The long-range trend in these states appears to favor the Republicans, but until recently the Democrats have been so powerful that the real contest over political principles and ideas usually occurred in the liberal-conservative factionalism within their party, which persisted in a fairly clear-cut manner for generations. In effect, there were three parties in the border states: liberal Democrats, Bourbon Democrats, and Republicans. But more and more of the conservative Democrats seem to find it desirable to shift over to the Republican party. At the same time, both parties have found it necessary to appeal to the urban voters. The situation in the southern rim states would seem to be similar in many respects to the situation in the border states, say, at about 1900.

Out of the great sectional conflict and its aftermath southern political leaders forged the Solid South. Essentially a rural people of great ethnic homogeneity (excepting those of darker skins), the Southerners became an enduring and highly-conscious minority in the larger nation, bound together by their experiences in war and reconstruction, frequently lashed by the winds of an intense Negrophobia, and sustained by the myth of the Old South and the narcissistic symbolism of the Lost Cause and the struggle for home rule. The milieu thus created, when combined with more practical considerations involving economic decisions and the actual exercise of political power, made the region easily susceptible to the one-party domination of the southern black belts and commercial interests. By the end of the nineteenth century, conservative leaders had created a sectional devotion to the Democratic party that was the most remarkable phenomenon of its kind in American history.

Yet political leaders were never able to unify the region completely. The Populist revolt, the first major challenge to Bourbon control, significantly altered southern politics, even though it strengthened the average Southerner's loyalty to the Democratic party. Within the confines of the Democratic South, urban and middle-class reform, Wilsonian liberalism, and the "business progressivism" of the 1920's mirrored important developments in the nation as a whole and indicated that a competitive politics was not impossible below the Potomac. The New Deal ushered in another period of stress and strain for the conservatives who usually dominated southern politics. By nationalizing most issues, by liberating the Democratic party from the dictation of southern leaders, and by bringing to political consciousness elements in the region which had long been unable to exert any influence in politics, the New Deal threatened the old power structure and nourished forces that eventually began to reconstruct the region's political affairs. Ultimately, profound changes of an economic and social nature within the region joined with compelling forces of national and international origin to give the old social and economic groupings new meaning and gradually to bring about a political realignment.

The southern experience demonstrates the fact that one-party politics offers a poor substitute for a two-party system. Class and group conflict easily become blurred; a dual factionalism based on liberal-conservative divisions has difficulty in perpetuating itself; and even though social conflict and ideological differences of a political character are to be found on every hand, it is not easy for them to be translated into desirable legislation or administrative action. Yet even under the domination of a single party, competition reflecting the realities of economic environment, social stratification, and demographic change has usually been found in the South's politics, waxing and waning, occasionally turning violent, but never quite disappearing. This competition has provided the basis for most of the positive political action and social reform on the state and local levels in the region. It has also made some contribution to a more diversified southern participation in Congress and national politics.

Southern politics may look like a crazy quilt. But the pattern has some logic, and the rich hues and contrasting colors remind one of the conflict and diversity that run strongly through southern history. The dominant pattern is the region's habit of conservatism, strengthened by recent economic developments. But there is also another pattern—less conspicuous but no less clearly defined—and it is the South's liberal tradition, a "strain of protest and experimentation in the search for economic equality."*

Southerners who are interested in such ironies may have the dubious satisfaction of knowing that the Solid South has served, however unwittingly, as the nation's political conscience. For the South has provided in bold relief and for over a century the best example of the flaunting of the nation's most hallowed political traditions: the two-party system, the expression of minority and dissenting views, and responsible and broadly representative political leadership. Surely there is no better candidate for the historic role of America's political pariah.

Yet the dialogue the South has carried on with the larger nation has probably confused Americans more than

---

*"The tragedy of the South," says Dean Acheson, "has been that racism has corrupted an otherwise respectable strain of protest and experimentation in the search for economic equality, dating back to Jefferson, Mason, Randolph, and Jackson." *A Democrat Looks at His Party* (New York, 1955), p. 44.

it has illuminated and strengthened the national traditions. For the dialogue has frequently brought a polariza-
tion of attitudes high above the field of actual politics
between a mystical national tradition and an alleged sectional aberration. Thus it has helped to conceal the real
dialectical process between the national government and
the southern states, as well as the extent to which Southerners have acted like other Americans, on the one hand,
and the extent to which non-Southerners have been aberrant (even like Southerners!) in terms of the nation's
ideals, on the other. A mixture of regional and national
loyalties, to use David M. Potter's phrase, has prevailed in
both North and South.

We are perhaps less innocent than we once were about
the difficulty of realizing the promise of our political traditions—in the South and in all parts of the country. But
all Americans who value those traditions may be encouraged, I think, by the unknown or largely forgotten lessons
from the chapter we have just surveyed in American political history. It reveals a South we know too little—the democratic South—frequently repressed but always struggling
and, we may fervently hope, growing stronger with the
passing of time.

Also see two articles on social stratification: Wilbert E. Moore and Robin M. Williams, "Stratification in the Ante-bellum South," *American Sociological Review,* VII (June, 1942), 343-51, and Rudolf Heberle, "The Changing Social Stratification of the South," *Social Forces,* XXXVIII (October, 1959), 42-50. Rupert B. Vance's *Human Geography of the South: A Study of Regional Resources and Human Adequacy* (1932) is an indispensable socio-economic guide to the region.

The best account of constitutional development and democratic advance in the Old South is contained in these writings of Fletcher M. Green: *Constitutional Development in the South Atlantic States, 1776-1860: A Study in the Evolution of Democracy* (1930); "Democracy in the Old South," *Journal of Southern History,* XII (February, 1946), 3-23; and "Cycles of American Democracy," *Mississippi Valley Historical Review,* XLVIII (June, 1961), 3-23. For a history of democracy in the country as a whole during this period, see Gilman Ostrander, *The Rights of Man in America, 1607-1861* (1960). A provocative work that throws a great deal of light on the unsuccessful southern search in the ante-bellum period for a new and non-American philosophy is Louis Hartz's study of the Lockeian tradition in the United States, *The Liberal Tradition in America: An Interpretation of American Political Thought since the Revolution* (1955). A good treatment of the Jacksonian movement in a single southern state is Edwin Arthur Miles, *Jacksonian Democracy in Mississippi* (1960). Virginius Dabney's *Liberalism in the South* (1932) attempts to demonstrate the venerability and continuity of liberal currents in the South. Charles Grier Sellers, Jr. (ed.), *The Southerner As American* (1960), emphasizes the Southerner's continuous involvement in the nation's evolving politics and ideology. The apparent paradox involved in the South's strong sectionalism and its continuing devotion to American nationalism is resolved in David M. Potter's penetrating critique of "The Historian's Use of Nationalism and Vice Versa, " *American Historical Review,* LXVII (July, 1962), 924-50. Potter argues that the cultural differences between the North and the South were insufficient to make possible a genuine southern nationalism, and that the growing southern sectionalism after 1846 can best be explained in terms of the conflict of interests in which the southern states found their own objectives increasingly jeopardized in the national arena. "By stressing conflict of interest as a basic factor," he writes, "it is possible to explain the otherwise stubborn anomaly that the sectional crisis grew in intensity even as the Republic grew in homogeneity."

A fresh and revealing interpretation of the Whigs in the Old South can be found in an article by Charles Grier Sellers, Jr., "Who Were the Southern Whigs?" *American Historical Review*, LIX (January, 1954), 335-46. For evidence of the social and geographical divisions in the South during the secession crisis, see Ralph A. Wooster, *The Secession Conventions of the South* (1962). For new light on Reconstruction, consult the perspicacious essay by Bernard A. Weisberger, "The Dark and Bloody Ground of Reconstruction Historiography," *Journal of Southern History*, XXV (November, 1959), 427-47, and the following writings: John Hope Franklin, *Reconstruction: After the Civil War* (1961); David H. Donald, "The Scalawag in Mississippi Reconstruction," *Journal of Southern History*, X (November, 1944), 447-60; T. Harry Williams, "The Louisiana Unification Movement of 1873," *ibid.*, XI (August, 1945), 349-69; Jack B. Scroggs, "Southern Reconstruction: A Radical View," *ibid.*, XXIV (November, 1958), 407-29; and Scroggs, "Carpetbagger Constitutional Reform in the South Atlantic States, 1867-1868," *ibid.*, XXVII (November, 1961), 475-93.

II. *The Forging of the Solid South*

The best treatment of the ante-bellum origins of southern sectionalism is Charles S. Sydnor's *The Development of Southern Sectionalism, 1819-1848* (1948). For the 1850's, see the comprehensive volume by Avery O. Craven, *The Growth of Southern Nationalism, 1848-1861* (1953). *Romance and Realism in Southern Politics* (1961), by T. Harry Williams, suggests that the Southerner's penchant for the romantic and the irrelevant contributed to the region's political unity. On this point and other intangibles, the student will also be indebted to W. J. Cash for his brilliant probing of the southern mystique, in *The Mind of the South* (1941). William R. Taylor's *Cavalier and Yankee: The Old South and American National Character* (1961) is a splendid study of the Cavalier-Yankee theme in the ante-bellum period and a suggestive critique of a myth that contributed to southern solidarity. For the Lost Cause, see the thoughtful essay by Robert Penn Warren, *The Legacy of the Civil War: Meditations on the Centennial* (1961).

The democratic tendencies of the Confederacy and their injurious effects upon the South's bid for independence are discussed in a suggestive essay by David Donald, "Died of Democracy," in Donald (ed.), *Why the North Won the Civil War* (1960), 77-90. Thomas B. Alexander has written a series of important articles on the persistence of Whiggery after 1861: "Whiggery and Reconstruction in Tennessee," *Journal of Southern History*, XVI (August, 1950), 291-305; "Persistent Whiggery in Alabama and the Lower South, 1860-1867," *Alabama Review*, XII (January, 1959), 35-52; "Persistent Whiggery in Mississippi: The Hinds County Gazette," *Journal of Mississippi History*, XXIII (April, 1961), 71-93; and "Persistent Whiggery in the Confederate South, 1860-1877," *Journal of Southern History*, XXVII (August, 1961), 305-29. Evidence of the significance of Whig strength during the Confederacy can also be found in Wilfred Buck Yearns, *The Confederate Congress* (1960). Frank Wysor Klingberg, *The Southern Claims Commission: A Study in Unionism* (Berkeley, 1955), suggests the importance of Unionist sentiment in the Confederacy. For the state rights controversies in the Confederacy, see E. Merton Coulter, *The Confederate States of America, 1861-1865* (1950). The pioneering work on the role of the old-line Whigs in the disputed election of 1876 is C. Vann Woodward's *Reunion and Reaction: The Compromise of 1877 and the End of Reconstruction* (1951).

No one can afford to overlook the brilliant writings of Professor Woodward on the post-Reconstruction period of southern history. His *Origins of the New South, 1877-1913* (1951) is not only a sparkling general history of an era but also a perceptive analysis of southern ideas and institutions. For good illustrations of Bourbon Democracy, see Allen Johnston Going, *Bourbon Democracy in Alabama, 1874-1890* (1951); Judson Clements Ward, Jr., "The New Departure Democrats of Georgia: An Interpretation," *Georgia Historical Quarterly*, XLI (September, 1957), 227-36; and Willie D. Halsell, "The Bourbon Period in Mississippi Politics, 1875-1890," *Journal of Southern History*, XI (November, 1945), 519-37.

The best treatment of southern Republicanism during the last quarter of the nineteenth century is Vincent P. De Santis, *Republicans Face the Southern Question—The New Departure Years, 1877-1897* (1959). Stanley P. Hirshson's *Farewell to the Bloody Shirt: Northern Republicans & the Southern Negro, 1877-1893* (1962) complements the work of De Santis and provides a good analysis of northern Republican attitudes toward the southern Negro during this period. Republican election percentages in this period were compiled from W. Dean Burnham, *Presidential Ballots, 1836-1892* (1955), and *Historical Statistics of the United States: Colonial Times to 1957* (1960). On the Readjuster Movement, see Charles Chilton Pearson, *The Readjuster Movement in Virginia* (1917), and Nelson Morehouse Blake, *William Mahone of Virginia: Soldier and Political Insurgent* (1935).

One of the best approaches to the agrarian revolt in the South is through biographies, of which the most useful are C. Vann Woodward, *Tom Watson: Agrarian Rebel* (1938); Francis Butler Simkins, *Pitchfork Ben Tillman: South Carolinian* (1944); Stuart Noblin, *Leonidas LaFayette Polk: Agrarian Crusader* (1949); Daniel Merritt Robison, *Bob Taylor and the Agrarian Revolt in Tennessee* (1935); Robert C. Cotner, *James Stephen Hogg: A Biography* (1959). Two of the best state studies are Alex Mathews Arnett, *The Populist Movement in Georgia: A View of the "Agrarian Crusade" in the Light of Solid-South Politics* (1922), and Roscoe C. Martin, *The People's Party in Texas: A Study in Third Party Politics* (1933). Theodore Saloutos, *Farmer Movements in the South, 1865-1933* (1960), is a work of major importance. An illuminating essay on "The Populist Heritage and the Intellectual" is contained in C. Vann Woodward's *The Burden of Southern History* (1960). For the fusion movement in North Carolina, see Helen G. Edmonds, *The Negro and Fusion Politics in North Carolina, 1894-1901* (1951).

III. *The One-Party South in Mid-Passage*

Many of my impressions about the course of the South during the first three decades of the twentieth century have been gained from extensive research in manuscript collections, newspaper files, and periodical literature. I have also benefited a great deal from reading several unpublished dissertations and theses dealing with various aspects of this period.

A first-rate monograph devoted to a single southern state during these years is Albert D. Kirwan's *Revolt of the Rednecks, Mississippi Politics: 1876-1925* (1951). A pioneering appraisal of southern progressivism is Arthur S. Link's article, "The Progressive Movement in the South, 1870-1914," *North Carolina Historical Review*, XXIII (April, 1946), 172-95. Among the biographies that treat southern progressive leaders are Samuel Proctor, *Napoleon Bonaparte Broward: Florida's Fighting Democrat* (1950); Oliver H. Orr, Jr., *Charles Brantley Aycock* (1961); and Dewey W. Grantham, Jr., *Hoke Smith and the Politics of the New South* (1958). For an able account of the railroad regulatory issue in one southern state, see James F. Doster, *Railroads in Alabama Politics, 1875-1914* (1957). Two useful studies of the prohibition movement in the South are James Benson Sellers, *The Prohibition Movement in Alabama, 1702 to 1943* (1943), and Daniel Jay Whitener, *Prohibition in North Carolina, 1715-1945* (1945).

Arthur S. Link has published a series of illuminating articles in southern historical journals on the Wilson movement in the South. Most of these were taken from his Ph.D. dissertation prepared at the University of North Carolina, "The South and the Democratic Campaign of 1912" (1945), and are summarized in the first volume of his biography of Wilson, *The Road to the White House* (1947). For the southern contribution to Wilsonian liberalism during the years 1913-1917, see Link's article, "The South and the 'New Freedom': An Interpretation," *American Scholar*, XX (Summer, 1951), 314-24. This interpretation has been challenged by Richard M. Abrams, "Woodrow Wilson and the Southern Congressmen, 1913-1916," *Journal of Southern History*, XXII (November, 1956), 417-37. Southern conservatism in Congress is also revealed in Howard W. Allen, "Geography and Politics: Voting on Reform Issues in the United States Senate, 1911-1916," *ibid.*, XXVII (May, 1961), 216-28.

The political odyssey of Josephus Daniels is described in great detail in his five-volume autobiography, and especially in the three volumes that cover the years 1893-1923: *Editor in Politics* (1941); *The Wilson Era: Years of Peace—1910-1917* (1944); and *The Wilson Era: Years of War and After, 1917-*

1923 (1946). See also Jonathan Daniels, *The End of Inno-cence* (1954), and two articles by E. David Cronon: "Josephus Daniels as a Reluctant Candidate," *North Carolina Historical Review,* XXXIII (October, 1956), 457-82, and "A Southern Progressive Looks at the New Deal," *Journal of Southern History,* XXIV (May, 1958), 151-76.

The best interpretation of progressivism in the South dur-ing the 1920's is George B. Tindall's article, "Business Progres-sivism: Southern Politics in the Twenties," *South Atlantic Quarterly,* LXII (Winter, 1963), 92-106. For another example, see William E. Gilbert, "Bibb Graves as a Progressive, 1927-1930," *Alabama Review,* X (January, 1957), 15-30. For Huey P. Long, see the suggestive article by T. Harry Williams, "The Gentleman from Louisiana: Demagogue or Democrat," *Jour-nal of Southern History,* XXVI (February, 1960), 3-21, and Allan P. Sindler, *Huey Long's Louisiana: State Politics, 1920-1952* (1956). The persistence of historic cleavages in two states is revealed in Sindler's article, "Bifactional Rivalry as an Alter-native to Two-Party Competition in Louisiana," *American Political Science Review,* XLIX (September, 1955), 641-62, and Herbert J. Doherty, Jr., "Liberal and Conservative Voting Patterns in Florida," *Journal of Politics,* XIV (August, 1952), 403-17.

The best brief account of the election of 1928 in the South is contained in Key's *Southern Politics in State and Nation.* Helpful for understanding the changing character of Demo-cratic politics in the country as a whole are Edmund A. Moore, *A Catholic Runs for President: The Campaign of 1928* (1956), and J. Joseph Huthmacher, *Massachusetts People and Politics, 1919-1933* (1959). For the experience of one southern leader, see Richard L. Watson, Jr., "A Political Leader Bolts—F. M. Simmons in the Presidential Election of 1928," *North Carolina Historical Review,* XXXVII (October, 1960), 516-43.

IV. *Tradition and New Departure*

There are as yet few scholarly studies of the New Deal's impact upon the South. But the periodical literature on south-ern politics during the 1930's and since is immense. Marian D. Irish's article, "The Proletarian South," *Journal of Politics,* II (August, 1940), 231-58, is suggestive. See also her essay, "The Southern One-Party System and National Politics," *ibid.,*

IV (February, 1942), 80-94. A sound monograph on the politics of one southern state during the early New Deal is Elmer L. Puryear, *Democratic Party Dissensions in North Carolina, 1928-1936* (1962). For the contribution of one moderate Southerner to the New Deal, read Walter J. Heacock, "William B. Bankhead and the New Deal," *Journal of Southern History*, XXI (August, 1955), 347-59.

The relationship between state rights and federal grants-in-aid to southern states is made admirably clear in Robert J. Harris, "States' Rights and Vested Interests," *Journal of Politics*, XV (November, 1953), 457-71. Samuel Lubell, *The Future of American Politics* (1952), is perceptive on the formation of the Roosevelt coalition and southern dissatisfaction with the New Deal. J. B. Shannon's two-part article, "Presidential Politics in the South: 1938," *Journal of Politics*, I (May and August, 1939), 146-70, 278-300, is useful. For insight into the thinking of a bitter southern critic of the New Deal, see Sarah McCulloh Lemmon, "The Ideology of Eugene Talmadge," *Georgia Historical Quarterly*, XXXVIII (September, 1954), 226-48.

Thomas D. Clark's sprightly volume, *The Emerging South* (1961), is valuable as a guide to the social and economic changes the region has experienced during the past forty years. For recent demographic changes, see John M. Maclachlan and Joe S. Floyd, Jr., *This Changing South* (1956). The impact of urbanization on the South is explored by a number of social scientists in Rupert B. Vance and Nicholas J. Demerath (eds.), *The Urban South* (1954). A monograph by Anthony M. Tang, *Economic Development in the Southern Piedmont, 1860-1950: Its Impact on Agriculture* (1958), suggests how a changing economy has affected the South's old-time agricultural system.

The Dixiecrat movement is analyzed in Key's *Southern Politics* and Alexander Heard's *A Two-Party South?* (1952). But also see William G. Carleton, "The Fate of Our Fourth Party," *Yale Review*, XXXVIII (Spring, 1949), 449-59; Emile B. Ader, "Why the Dixiecrats Failed," *Journal of Politics*, XV (August, 1953), 356-69; and Sarah McCulloh Lemmon, "The Ideology of the 'Dixiecrat' Movement," *Social Forces*, XXX (December, 1951), 162-71. For a provocative discussion of the persistence of southern sectionalism, see Fletcher M. Green, "Resurgent Southern Sectionalism, 1933-1955," *North Caro-*

lina Historical Review, XXXIII (April, 1956), 222-40. A comprehensive attempt to explain the role of the southern tradition in blocking the region's progress is William H. Nicholls, *Southern Tradition and Regional Progress* (1960).

The best treatment of modern Republicanism in the South is contained in Alexander Heard's *A Two-Party South?* Valuable for the light they throw on Republican victories in the South during the 1950's are these writings: Donald S. Strong, "The Presidential Election in the South, 1952," *Journal of Politics,* XVII (August, 1955), 343-89, and *Urban Republicanism in the South* (1960); Paul T. David, Malcolm Moos, and Ralph M. Goldman (eds.), *Presidential Nominating Politics in 1952: The South* (1954); James W. Prothro, Ernest Q. Campbell, and Charles M. Grigg, "Two-Party Voting in the South: Class Vs. Party Identification," *American Political Science Review,* LII (March, 1958), 131-39; and Bernard Cosman, "Presidential Republicanism in the South, 1960," *Journal of Politics,* XXIV (May, 1962), 303-22. See also Rudolf Heberle, George Hillery, Jr., and Frank Lovrich, "Continuity and Change in Voting Behavior in the 1952 Primaries in Louisiana," *Southwestern Social Science Quarterly,* XXXIII (March, 1953), 328-42. Republican voting percentages during the last decade were compiled from Richard M. Scammon (comp. and ed.), *America Votes: A Handbook of Contemporary American Election Statistics* (4 vols., 1956-1962).

The following works are helpful in gaining some understanding of the so-called southern Democratic-Republican coalition in Congress: Julius Turner, *Party and Constituency: Pressures on Congress* (1951); George L. Grassmuck, *Sectional Biases in Congress on Foreign Policy* (1951); and an unsigned article, "How Big Is the North-South Democratic Split?", *Congressional Quarterly Almanac,* 85 Cong., 1 Sess. (1957), XIII, 813-17. For the changing position of southern congressmen on the tariff and other international questions, see Richard A. Watson, "The Tariff Revolution: A Study of Shifting Party Attitudes," *Journal of Politics,* XVIII (November, 1956), 678-701, and Charles O. Lerche, Jr., "Southern Congressmen and the 'New Isolationism,'" *Political Science Quarterly,* LXXV (September, 1960), 321-37.

The return of Negroes to the polls in the South and the obstacles that continue to prevent many of them from voting may be followed in Margaret Price, *The Negro Voter in the South* (Special Report of the Southern Regional Council, 1957); H. D. Price, *The Negro and Southern Politics: A Chapter of Florida History* (1957); Louis E. Lomax, *The Negro Revolt* (1962) ; and a valuable symposium, "The Negro Voter in the South," *Journal of Negro Education,* XXVI (Summer, 1957), 213-431. For the Negro voter in the nation at large, see Henry Lee Moon, *Balance of Power: The Negro Vote* (1948), and James Q. Wilson, *Negro Politics: The Search for Leadership* (1960).

Anyone who surveys the writings on recent southern politics will be impressed by the contributions of American political scientists. In addition to the works mentioned above, the following are especially noteworthy: Taylor Cole and John H. Hollowell (eds.) , *The Southern Political Scene* (1948) ; Jasper Berry Shannon, *Toward a New Politics in the South* (1949); Cortez A. M. Ewing, *Primary Elections in the South: A Study in Uniparty Politics* (1953); and Joseph L. Bernd, *Grass Roots Politics in Georgia: The County Unit System and the Importance of the Individual Voting Community in Bifactional Elections, 1942-1954* (1960). Three perceptive articles that should be mentioned are H. C. Nixon, "Politics of the Hills," *Journal of Politics,* VIII (May, 1946) , 123-33; William G. Carleton, "Why Call the South Conservative?", *Harper's Magazine,* CXCV (July, 1947), 61-68; and Marian D. Irish, "Political Thought and Political Behavior in the South," *Western Political Quarterly,* XIII (June, 1960), 406-20. Alexander Heard and Donald S. Strong (eds.), *Southern Primaries and Elections, 1920-1949* (1950), contains valuable data for the study of recent southern politics. For the border states, see John H. Fenton, *Politics in the Border States: A Study of the Patterns of Political Organization, and Political Change, Common to the Border States—Maryland, West Virginia, Kentucky and Missouri* (1957). An able discussion of comparative state politics in the United States is V. O. Key, Jr., *American State Politics: An Introduction* (1956).

Among the large number of more popular books devoted to southern politics or general regional development, the following are particularly important: Virginius Dabney, *Below the Potomac: A Book About the New South* (1942); Harry S. Ashmore, *An Epitaph for Dixie* (1957) ; Wilma Dykeman and

James Stokely, *Neither Black Nor White* (1957); James McBride Dabbs, *The Southern Heritage* (1958); Henry Savage, Jr., *Seeds of Time: The Background of Southern Thinking* (1959); and Benjamin Muse, *Virginia's Massive Resistance* (1961).

American History Titles in
THE NORTON LIBRARY